M A I

The Multilateral Agreement on Investment and the Threat to Canadian Sovereignty

TONY CLARKE and MAUDE BARLOW

Published in 1997 by Stoddart Publishing Co. Limited
34 Lesmill Road, Toronto, Canada M3B 2T6
Tel. (416) 445-3333 Fax (416) 445-5967
Email Customer.Service@ccmailgw.genpub.com

01 00 99 98 97 1 2 3 4 5

Stoddart Books are available for bulk purchase for sales promotions, premiums, fundraising, and seminars. For details, contact the Special Sales Department at the above address.

Canadian Cataloguing in Publication Data

Clarke, Tony
MAI: the Multilateral Agreement on Investment and the
threat to Canadian sovereignty

Includes index.
ISBN 0-7737-5946-8

1. Investments, Foreign – Canada. 2. Corporations, Foreign – Canada.
3. Investments, Foreign – Social aspects – Canada.
4. International business enterprises. I. Barlow, Maude. II. Title.

HG5152.C52 1997   332.67'3'0971   C97-932316-9

Cover design: Pekoe Jones
Text design & page composition: Tannice Goddard

Printed and bound in Canada

*We gratefully acknowledge the Canada Council for the Arts and the
Ontario Arts Council for their support of our publishing program.*

To our international colleagues and fellow trade warriors
Martin Khor, Lori Wallach, John Cavanagh,
Vandana Shiva, Sara Larrain, Bertha Luhan,
Jane Kelsey, and Mark Ritchie with love

CONTENTS

ACKNOWLEDGEMENTS

There is a whole community of friends and colleagues who have encouraged us in the writing of this book. We would particularly like to thank readers Bruce Campbell, Elizabeth May, John Dillon, Andrew Jackson, Paul Audley, Keith Kelly, and Steve Shrybman for their recommendations, guidance, and support. The staff at the Council of Canadians has been enormously helpful and patient with us. Special thanks to Patricia Armstrong and Joanne Polsky for all their hard work.

We are grateful as well to Jack Stoddart for his leadership in the protection of Canadian culture and for coming up with the idea for this book. The whole team at Stoddart has been wonderful. Particular appreciation to editor Marnie Kramarich who worked on such a tight timeline with grace and humour. To our families, especially Carol and Andrew, many thanks for your continued support.

SETTING THE SCENE

There comes a time when citizens who are deeply involved in struggles for democratic social change in Canada need to step back, reflect on their experience, and recharge their batteries. For us, that moment came in January 1994 following eight long years of fighting the battle against free trade: first the Free Trade Agreement (FTA) between Canada and the United States, then the North American Free Trade Agreement (NAFTA), which included Mexico.

This moment also turned out to be a turning point. In the wake of the final vote on NAFTA in the U.S. Congress, environmental activist Jerry Mander invited us to join people involved in social movements around the world — in Asia, Africa, and Latin America as well as Europe and North America — to share what they had learned in confronting free trade and related forms of economic globalization. The gathering called itself the International Forum on Globalization.

It was through this forum, during the following year, that we first learned about the Multilateral Agreement on Investment

1

(MAI). Martin Khor of the Third World Network was among the first to warn that negotiations to establish a global investment regime were being initiated behind closed doors in Paris at the Organisation for Economic Co-operation and Development (OECD) and simultaneously at the newly formed World Trade Organization (WTO).

A cloud of secrecy hung over the negotiations. The U.S. was known to be the driving force behind the OECD negotiations, while the European Union was spearheading the talks at the WTO. U.S. trade activist Lori Wallach of Public Citizen, the influential citizens' lobby led by Ralph Nader, began to probe developments in Washington, D.C., while others started digging up whatever information they could find about the new treaty.

Here at home, we began to do our own homework with a network of colleagues who had been active as researchers during the free trade battles. It soon became clear that Canada was by no means an innocent bystander in these secret negotiations. In the Chrétien government, former trade minister Roy MacLaren had paved the way for Ottawa to play a pivotal role in selling the idea of a global investment treaty, especially to Third World countries.

At the same time, academics like Alan Rugman from the University of Toronto's School of Business and Michael Hart of Carleton University's Centre for Trade Policy and Law were identified as two of the initial architects of the global investment deal. Rugman himself had prepared a background study for the OECD on the need for such a treaty before the current round of negotiations began in 1995.

In January 1997 the OECD began circulating a confidential draft of the MAI. Through our network of researchers, we began an extensive search for the MAI draft text here in Canada. One lead followed another and before we knew it, in early March, we had the confidential document in our hands. Our strategy was threefold: first, study the text; second, make it public; third, circulate it worldwide.

By early April, we had prepared a preliminary analysis of the MAI that was subsequently published by the Canadian Centre for Policy Alternatives under the title *The Corporate Rule Treaty.* On April 3, news of the MAI draft document was publicly released for the first time in the world through a front page story in *The Globe and Mail.* At the same time, we arranged to have the full text of the document scanned and put on the Internet through the *Multinational Monitor* in Washington, D.C.

Although these events occurred on the eve of the 1997 Canadian federal election, it was not our objective to make the MAI a major election issue. Experience had shown that it takes several months' lead time to lay the groundwork on a particular issue before it can be expected to become the focal point of a general election. Instead, the objective was to surface the issue through newspaper ads and debates at all-candidates meetings.

But Canada's trade minister at the time, Art Eggleton, quickly patched together a pre-election defence plan. After the text was made public, his office fired off a memo inviting Liberal MPs to a closed-door MAI briefing session to discuss how to handle media reports that "raise the question of potential problems as to the sovereignty of Canada." Out on the hustings, Eggleton declared: "As far as I know — I'm sure somebody told me this not too long ago — we did not initiate this matter." He added that it was "too early" to give this matter public debate.

The MAI did surface as an issue during the election. Letters were sent to four cabinet ministers — Sheila Copps at heritage, John Manley at industry, Sergio Marchi at environment, and David Dingwall at health — sounding the alarm about the secret negotiations and the implications for their respective portfolios. The Council of Canadians published a national newspaper ad while groups of citizens took the issue to all-candidates meetings in dozens of ridings across the country. Towards the end of the campaign, the increasing volume of MAI-related questions being addressed to candidates prompted New Democrat leader Alexa McDonough to call a press conference on the MAI.

Since the election, however, senior trade officials seem to have done everything they can to keep the lid on any internal discussion of and public debate about the MAI. In order to control information, only a partial version of the text was circulated over the 1997 summer break to twelve government departments directly affected by the negotiations. Major sections of the official draft text were missing, including the clauses dealing with "roll-back," "standstill," and "lock-in," as well as the requirement that countries submit a "hit list" of legislation and programs that do not conform with the proposed MAI rules.

Meanwhile, briefing sessions with the provinces are under way and the Department of Foreign Affairs and International Trade is assembling a group of public relations experts to "sell" the MAI to Canadians. *But who will tell the people the truth about the MAI?*

This troubling question provoked us enough to put aside extremely busy schedules to write this book. What follows is not intended to be an in-depth analytical treatment of the MAI in all of its complexities. Our first and foremost concern has been to provide Canadians with a road map for understanding what this global investment treaty could mean for us in the future — especially our economic, social, cultural, environmental, and political rights as citizens in a democratic society.

It should be emphasized, however, that the MAI is not yet a done deal. While OECD officials claim that consensus has been reached on close to 90 percent of the text, negotiations are still continuing in Paris. Two official drafts of the treaty have surfaced so far in 1997, one in January, the other in May, with a third expected in October. Like the rest of the Canadian people, we have had to rely on leaked versions of the document to obtain the information required to prepare this book. Working with a moving target has certainly complicated our task; nevertheless, we have prepared an analysis based on the first two versions of the draft treaty, recognizing that further changes are likely. Yet, as they say, everything is still on the table until the deal is signed and sealed.*

Over the year ahead, public discussion and debate about the implications of the MAI for Canada's economy and society are bound to take shape. The formal approval-in-principle among the twenty-nine member countries of the OECD is not expected to take place until the ministerial meeting in May of 1998. Following this, the treaty must be ratified by the national legislatures of each country. In Canada, this will be done by Parliament passing "implementing legislation" designed to amend a series of existing laws to comply with the MAI.

We do not wish to leave the impression that we reject the idea of a global investment treaty. We are well aware that transnational investment flows have been accelerating at a rapid pace and that there is a need to establish some global rules. But the basic premise on which the draft versions of the MAI have been crafted is, in our view, largely flawed and one-sided. It expands the rights and powers of transnational corporations without imposing any corresponding obligations. Instead, the draft treaty places obligations squarely on the shoulders of governments,

---

* Readers wishing to examine the latest version of the draft MAI text may find it at the following web address: http://www.citizen.org/gtw/mai.html

outlining the rules they must follow to facilitate profitable transnational investment. Meanwhile, the MAI says nothing about the rules that transnational corporations must follow to respect the economic, social, cultural, and environmental rights of citizens.

We hope this book will help citizen movements to mobilize public participation in a debate that could have a profound effect on the destiny of Canada and, indeed, the rest of the world.

ONE

THE RISE AND FALL OF DEMOCRATIC RIGHTS

"It is horrible to see everything that one detested in the past coming back wearing the colours of the future."
— JEAN ROSTAND

In 1998, the nations of the world, including Canada, celebrate the fiftieth anniversary of the United Nations' historic Universal Declaration of Human Rights. This Declaration marked a watershed in the long international quest to assert the supremacy of human and citizen rights over political or economic tyranny of any kind. Together with the International Covenant on Economic, Social and Cultural Rights and the International Covenant on Civil and Political Rights, the Declaration stood and stands as a twentieth-century Magna Carta.

But in 1998, the richest nations of the world, including Canada, are also poised to ratify a treaty that will grant so much power to transnational corporations and stateless global capital

7

that the democratic rights granted to the peoples of the world by the UN Declaration will be seriously compromised. The Multilateral Agreement on Investment (MAI) is the culmination of a global assault, in the name of commercial freedom, on these social rights and on the commitments to ecological stewardship made by the world's nations at the 1992 Rio Earth Summit.

The MAI, if ratified, will serve as a Charter of Rights and Freedoms for transnational corporations against citizens and the earth, and represents a grave threat to democracy in Canada and around the world.

The Rise of Democratic Rights

In 1948, civilization had just passed through one of the bloodiest armed conflicts in history, a multi-faceted war during which humans visited upon other humans acts so barbarous they set a new standard in horror. The world vowed "never again," and put it in writing that year in the form of the Universal Declaration of Human Rights.

The Declaration broke new ground on many fronts. It granted fundamental human rights of freedom, equality, life, liberty, and security to every person, without distinction according to race, colour, sex, language, religion, political opinion, national or social origin, property, birth, or other status. It banned slavery, torture, arbitrary arrest, detention, and exile.

It affirmed the rights of nationality, freedom of thought, expression, and assembly, the right to vote, and the right to marry and rear a family. It declared equal rights for every person before the law and established the right of presumed innocence and a fair trial. It secured the rights of freedom of movement and asylum from persecution.

But the Declaration went a lot further. It also included what could be called rights of citizenship — those services and social protections that every citizen has a right to demand of his or her government. These rights include social security: everyone, as a member of society, "is entitled to realization, through national effort and international co-operation and in accordance with the organization and resources of each State, of the economic, social and cultural rights indispensable for his dignity and the free development of his personality."

Everyone, declared the United Nations, has the right to work, to just conditions of work, to equal pay, to just and favourable remuneration worthy of human dignity, to membership in a trade union, to rest and leisure, and to protection against unemployment. Everyone, by right of citizenship, is entitled to a standard of living adequate for the health and well-being of the whole family, including food, clothing, housing, medical care, and the right to security in the event of unemployment, sickness, disability, old age, or other circumstances that lead to a lack of livelihood and are beyond the citizen's control.

The fruits of scientific advancement must be shared by all, declared the UN, and everyone has the right to freely participate in the cultural life of the community. Protections were spelled out for women during and after pregnancy and all children, regardless of family status, were granted equal social protection. Everyone has the right to free, compulsory education, and education must be directed to promote understanding, racial and religious tolerance, friendship and peace among all nations, and the human rights contained in the Declaration.

The Covenants, which were later ratified by most governments, bound the state signatories (including Canada) to accept a moral and legal obligation to protect and promote the human

9

and democratic rights delineated in the Declaration and contained the measures of implementation required to do so. Where the Declaration was meant to enshrine the human rights of people everywhere, regardless of their governments' commitment or behaviour, the Covenants were meant to bind nation-states to the active preservation of these rights.

The individual rights and responsibilities of citizens — as established in the Declaration — together with the collective rights and responsibilities of nation-states — as established in the Covenants — together came to represent the foundation stones of democracy in the modern world. But the right of national governments to play a role by, for example, legislating policies and programs of full employment, universal social programs, and cultural protections, is now threatened by the forces of economic globalization; in particular, by the MAI.

The UN Universal Declaration of Human Rights and the Covenants were the basis for a global crusade to establish universal health and education programs. The Declaration was the springboard for the global war on child poverty and the model for the United Nations' Declaration on the Rights of the Child in 1959, and the Convention on the Rights of the Child, adopted in 1990. The World Health Organization's campaigns to eradicate infectious disease and infant mortality were also inspired by the Declaration.

The Declaration served as the template for Canada's social programs and coincided with this country's own transformation to a "social" nation-state, one in which all Canadian citizens had equal access to universal education, health care, pensions, social assistance, and unemployment insurance. Canada also modelled its domestic policy on the Declaration's commitment to decent wages, working conditions, and full employment.

Developing countries used the UN Declaration and the Covenants in negotiating protections for their industries, natural resources, and agricultural products in trade agreements; it was largely understood that nation-states, in order to protect both their political sovereignty and their citizens' social and employment rights as set out in the Declaration, had to maintain state regulatory tools. In particular, nation-states placed conditions on foreign investment and foreign ownership of land and natural resources. The constitutions of many countries contained provisions to control the admission and activity of foreign investment over vital national sectors of the economy.

Canada, too, had built up a regulatory framework to protect our resources, culture, and social programs. Living next to the world's largest superpower, Canada had become the most foreign-controlled developed country in the world; Canada's development as a nation-state included government protections (often very weak) of vulnerable industries such as transportation, communications, and financial services, as well as the screening of foreign investment, regulation of foreign access to energy and water, and the maintenance of domestic content rules in culture, telecommunications, education, and the media. Public social programs, including medicare, were strictly off-limits to foreign ownership.

The Threat to Democratic Rights

However, parallel to the United Nations' post-war process to develop an international regime of citizen and nation-state democracy, another, very different, process was being launched. Economic globalization was beginning on a number of fronts, and it offered an alternative and very different vision for the future of humanity.

The United States has long advocated an open global investment regime in order to advance the interests of its corporations. After World War II, that country found itself with a highly industrialized infrastructure producing more goods than it needed for its own consumers. At the same time, the U.S. assumed the role of global defender of the "free market," and took on the task of defeating communism and socialism everywhere it might be found.

The United States set about the rebuilding of Europe with its massive Marshall Plan — a military and economic project built on a market model. It also brought together the world's financial elite in the small New Hampshire town of Bretton Woods in 1944 to set the post-war conditions for global economic recovery, and established the Bretton Woods institutions: the World Bank, to assist developing countries with long-term development programs, and the International Monetary Fund (IMF), to promote currency stability and liberalization of international trade. While development and the alleviation of poverty were the stated goals of the Bretton Woods institutions, the underlying mandate became the expansion and integration of a global financial system and market mirrored on the U.S. economic model.

These initiatives together created massive markets for American goods and profits for U.S. business unrivalled in the history of the world. As journalist Linda McQuaig notes, "Essentially, the U.S. government was using U.S. taxpayers' money to create prosperity — a prosperity that was based on the growth and dominance of U.S. corporations."

In 1947 Washington also scuttled moves to establish an international trade regime that would have obliged member countries to incorporate the provisions of the UN Declaration, setting standards for full employment, working conditions, and social security. More ominously for American corporate interests, this agreement would have allowed a country to expropriate the assets of a foreign company for reasons of national economic sovereignty. The U.S. refused to even present the charter of the newly formed International Trade Organization to Congress, thereby sounding its death knell. It chose instead to create, in 1948, the General Agreement on Tariffs and Trade (GATT), a body that would concentrate on opening up world markets for U.S. goods by reducing tariff barriers on goods and services.

Until the 1980s, the United States attempted to establish foreign investment rules inside the United Nations itself. However, the UN proved too democratic in its structure and too concerned with democracy as a principle to provide the protection U.S. corporations were seeking.

In 1974, under the influence of the developing nations, the UN enacted a Charter of Economic Rights and Duties of States, which stated that member nations have the "inalienable right" to "regulate and exercise authority over foreign investment" and that "no State shall be compelled to grant preferential treatment to foreign investment." It granted nations the right to "regulate and supervise the activities of transnational corporations" in the national interest, including performance requirements, and declared that "transnational corporations shall not intervene in the internal affairs of the host State." As well, the code allowed member states to "nationalize, expropriate or transfer ownership of foreign property." While it stated that fair compensation should be paid in cases of expropriation, it allowed the country in question to determine the amount, taking into account its own needs. The United States voted against this charter. Canada abstained.

The UN also set up the United Nations Centre on Transnational Corporations in the late 1970s, and drafted a Code of

Conduct to regulate corporate behaviour. (This came about after it became public that International Telephone and Telegraph proposed to protect its interests in Chile by financing a campaign by the U.S. Central Intelligence Agency to defeat the candidacy of Salvador Allende in Chile's national election.) The United States looked to greener pastures for the rules it was seeking.

The Washington Consensus

Over the past few decades, the discrediting and eventual collapse of communism provided fertile ground for an emerging global regime based on an ideology that places the needs of capital and corporations above the needs and rights of nation-states and their citizens. This ideology is fundamentally opposed to the notion of citizen and nation-state democracy contained in the UN Declaration — a notion the powerful Trilateral Commission called "an excess of democracy" in a 1970s paper. (The Trilateral Commission is a global forum of CEOs and leaders of the major industrialized countries formed in the early 1970s to dismantle the Keynesian model of the nation-state and to reform and restructure the global economy. Originally created by David Rockefeller, chairman of Chase Manhattan Bank, and Zbigniew Brzezinski, who would become national security advisor to U.S. president Jimmy Carter, the commission grew to include 325 top leaders, CEOs, government bureaucrats, academics, and members of the media.) The philosophy of the Trilateralists has come to be known as the "Washington Consensus," a model of development based on the belief that liberal market economics is the one and only economic hope for all countries, including poor countries.

According to this doctrine, governments have to be prepared to give up their controls on foreign investment and prepare their citizens for competitive labour conditions and privatized social security. Foreign investment, unimpeded by conditions and built on cheap labour, will eventually bring prosperity. With time, labour and human rights issues may get addressed, but building a free market economy without restrictions must be the first priority. The Washington Consensus has also been called "democracy delayed" because the democratic citizens' rights that form the heart of the UN Declaration are largely absent from this model. Most important, it seeks the political stability so crucial to global investors and their nation-state patrons.

The Washington Consensus, economist Paul Krugman explains, now defines "not only the U.S. government, but all those institutions and networks of opinion leaders centred in the world's de facto capital — think tanks, politically sophisticated investment bankers, and worldly finance ministers, all those who meet each other in Washington and collectively define the conventional wisdom of the moment." This Consensus is disseminating a political monoculture, a single world view. It is, quite simply, the globalization of an ideology, a world economic order designed by and for capital exporters.

The globalization of this ideology required two conditions: the technology to create a borderless economic system and the political co-operation of national governments to establish a set of globally recognized rules to protect investors.

As technology advanced, the first condition was met. Big business went global. Two decades ago, the UN reported that there were approximately 7,000 transnational corporations in the world; today, there are more than 40,000. The top 200, reports the Washington-based Institute for Policy Studies, are so large and powerful that together their annual sales are bigger than the combined economies of 182 of the 191 countries in the world, and equal to almost twice the total income of the lowest-earning four-fifths of humanity. These corporations and the political coalitions they have formed have placed relentless pressure on nation-states to abandon economic and cultural protectionism and adopt rules necessary for their long-term prosperity.

The second condition, political co-operation to set rules, not surprisingly found its first adherents in the industrialized nations that housed these transnational corporations. The Organisation for Economic Co-operation and Development (OECD) is made up of the twenty-nine most powerful economies on earth. In the 1970s, the member states were all dominated by large capital exporters and consequently shared U.S. hostility to the continued insistence of the developing world to set conditions upon foreign investment.

The seeds of the MAI were planted in the OECD in the 1960s, when member countries adopted two binding codes on investment liberalization: the Code of Liberalization of Capital Movements and the Code of Liberalization of Current Invisible Operations. (Canada was the sole hold-out member on these codes and remained so until the early 1980s.) A third, non-binding code on "national treatment" — the requirement to grant the corporations of another member country the same rights as domestic producers — was adopted in 1973. The stated desire was to "put a fence around the use of governmental policies that distort patterns of investment and trade."

While these codes set the stage for later developments, they were far narrower in scope than the U.S. wanted. Further, the absence of a supranational legal institution to enforce them meant that adherence was spotty, relying on peer pressure to encourage compliance. Perhaps the biggest drawback to the OECD was that the codes didn't apply to non-members — the majority of the world's nations, among whom were numbered the biggest transgressors of free trade and investment liberalization. In fact, protectionist sentiment was growing in the Third World. The U.S. started to look to the GATT to develop a more comprehensive set of rules that would bind many more countries.

Meanwhile, developing countries were brought to heel by the Bretton Woods institutions, which used the countries' debt obligations to get them to weaken their tools of national sovereignty and to adopt a free market economic model. Massive loans at low interest rates were negotiated with commercial banks; when the interest rates skyrocketed, the World Bank and the IMF demanded deep structural adjustments to the internal policies of these nations in return for debt renegotiation.

Debt-laden countries such as Mexico and Zambia had to dramatically reduce the role and scope of government, slashing funding for public education, pensions, and health care; deregulating transportation, telecommunications, and utilities; lowering minimum wage and working standards; replacing traditional agriculture systems with corporate agribusiness to grow cash crops for export; and selling off state assets. Most important, barriers to foreign investment had to be removed. Domestic industry and farming were opened up to foreign competition. Barriers to unrestricted trade had to start coming down. Transnational investment and corporations were given preferential treatment over local business.

(In spite of all these sacrifices, Third World debt grew — by 400 percent between 1980 and 1995. Up until 1983, says the independent international development organization CUSO, the amount of capital that was transferred South, either as investments or in foreign aid, was greater than the amount of capital that was being sent North. Since then, the direction has reversed; Southern countries now send more money to the North as a condition of repaying their loans than they receive back. As a result, the national sovereignty of more than eighty countries that have undergone structural adjustment has been seriously eroded, as has their ability to maintain their social commitment to the UN Declaration. In almost every case, these nations have emerged poorer than they were before the process began. The UN says these countries have paid their debts with the health and lives of their children.)

The Growing Influence of Foreign Direct Investment

In the 1980s, the dramatic increase in global investment flows and the rapid ascension of foreign investment to a central place in the world economy added urgency to the push for an MAI. Since World War II, but especially in the last decade, global Foreign Direct Investment (FDI) has soared, mostly to the benefit of the industrialized countries. According to the Washington-based Institute for International Economics, FDI has grown by 80 percent over the last decade to become a more important part of the world's fixed capital formation, overtaking trade in goods and services.

In 1995, global sales of foreign affiliates of transnationals amounted to U.S.$7 trillion, well above the U.S.$5.8 trillion in world exports of goods and services. Trade across borders is less important than the investments that penetrate national boundaries. "Traditional trade liberalization won't do much for you any more," says University of Toronto international relations professor John Kirton, "unless you can have a rules-based regime for investment."

Until the early 1970s, the U.S. was the principal exporter; since then, it has maintained that status (in fact, annual outflow of FDI from the U.S. increased an astounding 785 percent in the last decade) and has also become the biggest importer. In spite of all the talk of investment benefits to developing countries, World Trade Organization (WTO) figures show that the so-called Triad countries, North America, Europe, and Japan, attracted 75 percent of FDI in the last ten years, even though they make up only 14 percent of the world population.

Other forms of investment are also growing dramatically. Pension and mutual funds have exploded. According to the 1997 *World Investment Report*, produced by the United Nations Committee on Trade and Development (UNCTAD), the total number of international emerging-country equity market funds, mainly mutual funds, grew from twenty-eight in 1986 to 1,435 in 1996, with the total net asset value of these funds rising from U.S.$2 billion to U.S.$135 billion. Deregulation of the global finance sector has triggered an explosion in currency speculation — about $2 trillion a day, mostly untouched by governments anywhere. Speculative investment, which far exceeds the combined resources available to the central banks of nation-states, now accounts for the vast majority of these transactions; most investment produces neither jobs nor goods.

But these forms of investment and FDI don't require the same sort of rules. According to the U.S. Department of Commerce, FDI "implies that a person in one country has a lasting interest in, and a degree of influence over, the management of a business enterprise in another country." In other words, unlike investment from a distance, or, for that matter, better access to trade by the transnational producers of goods and services, FDI requires market *presence*, a foothold, in the other country. Says the

European Union (EU), "To conquer a market, one must be present as a producer." For this, a stable investment environment with rules protecting the investor from political upheaval is crucial.

While the need for such protection is understandable and even desirable as long as foreign investors abide by acceptable environmental and labour standards, the staggering growth of FDI has created a climate that does more than just protect legitimate business interests. Corporate investors are now using their clout to shape global economic policy and to create rules that actually promote deregulation and more punitive conditions for workers.

The rapid growth of FDI and the growing power of transnational corporations have been mirrored by a strengthening of international movements concerned about the effects of trade and investment liberalization on citizens and the environment. These groups, including some powerful trade unions, oppose the Washington Consensus and pose a serious threat to its advancement. Their presence and growing strength have added a sense of urgency in the corporate quest for a binding treaty to protect capital investments. Rules for the protection of FDI have emerged as the top priority for transnational corporations and industrialized nations, particularly the United States.

The Birth of the MAI

The idea of a free-standing, enforceable multilateral investment agreement emerged during the GATT Uruguay Round negotiations in the mid-1980s. The GATT, unlike the OECD, provided for the enforcement of rules by sanctioned trade retaliation on the part of its members. It was, therefore, more binding than the OECD, and the GATT's members included developing countries, the very target of these rules. Because of their size, large market economies like the U.S., Japan, and Europe wield a major influence in the GATT; rather than lose market access to these bigger economies, smaller members carefully choose their policy tools to favour foreign investment.

The Uruguay Round of GATT brought 108 countries together to stem the growing tide of protectionism — which then chairman of American Express James Robinson III called "economic heroin" — in Third World countries. The key goals were to begin negotiations in two new arenas for the GATT: services, particularly financial services like banking, data processing, and insurance; and investment. Up until then, notwithstanding repeated attempts by the U.S. to enlarge its scope, the GATT had dealt largely in the trade of goods; the right to control financial services and foreign investment had been fiercely guarded by most nation-states, lying as they do at the very heart of a country's economic sovereignty.

In particular, through the GATT the U.S. was seeking rules to limit the ability of governments receiving foreign investment to impose performance requirements that would benefit the host country. Called TRIMs (trade-related investment measures), they might require a foreign corporation to invest in the local economy, hire locally, buy a certain amount of its inputs for a product from the host country, place a certain number of the country's citizens on the board of directors, balance exports and imports, or transfer technology in exchange for the privilege of being allowed to invest in the host country.

The issue of TRIMs was a matter of hot disagreement, with developing countries opposed to their inclusion in the GATT and the U.S., Europe, and Japan wanting an exhaustive list of restrictions on TRIMs. In the end, a compromise was reached, with a lowest common denominator TRIMs agreement imposed by the chair in 1991. While it was limited to trade in goods, the agreement did legitimize the GATT's right to set rules on FDI, and identified TRIMs as a violation of the spirit of the GATT, requiring all nations to list all non-conforming practices and set targets for their elimination.

The U.S. position at the GATT was strengthened by its newly minted free trade deals in North America. Both the 1989 Canada-U.S. Free Trade Agreement and NAFTA, signed in 1993, broke unprecedented ground in the disputed areas of financial services and investment. (In fact, American Express's James Robinson III was involved in initiating the bilateral deal with Canada; he knew that a precedent like this would serve as a model at the GATT and advance his interests in the multilateral arena.)

Under the FTA and NAFTA, Canada agreed to abandon the kinds of policies that had created the Foreign Investment Review Agency, which Brian Mulroney unilaterally disbanded in 1985. Most new American investment and acquisitions of Canadian companies (under $150 million) coming into Canada could no longer be screened, and Canada granted national treatment ("treatment no less favourable than that available to nationals within the investing state") to U.S. corporations, giving away many rights to favour Canadian companies. NAFTA prohibited the Canadian government from requiring an American company to achieve a level of domestic content, balance exports and imports, transfer technology to Canada, or keep any profits in Canada in exchange for locating here.

NAFTA also prohibited Canada from exacting an exit tax from American companies that shut down their profitable Canadian operations to relocate to a "sweatshop" location; and Canada cannot raise tariffs on these products when they reenter our markets. For example, the hands of the Canadian government were tied by these trade agreements when Nike recently took over and then relocated the Bauer skate plant in Cambridge, Ontario, to the Third World (after learning the technology of this highly competitive business and laying off 400 Canadian workers).

NAFTA also established the long-sought-after principle of "most favoured nation" status for corporations, which says that the investors and corporations of all the member signatories to a trade agreement must be given equal treatment and access, regardless of their labour, human rights, or environmental practices. In a smaller trade bloc like the current NAFTA, this provision has not had much attention; however, the global blocs that are forming include member countries with intolerable records in these areas.

One of NAFTA's most important precedent-setting elements was the establishment of stringent compensation standards in the event of an expropriation or nationalization, enforceable before international trade tribunals. That means that if the Canadian government wanted to protect old-growth forest already earmarked for clear-cutting by a foreign transnational, or set up a national, public day care program, it might have to pay compensation to foreign investors against lost potential future profits.

The investment rules of the free trade agreements were crucial to their success, for they bound Canada to U.S. investment interests forever. Any roll-back of these commitments would mean being shut out of the American market, a prospect that becomes bleaker as our economies merge and Canada becomes more dependent on the U.S. with every passing year.

These rules have been replicated in a series of bilateral investment treaties between countries. The UN reports that more than

1,160 of these bilateral treaties (BITs) had been negotiated by June 1996, two-thirds of them in the 1990s. Canada alone has signed eighteen Foreign Investment Protection Agreements and is negotiating four others, including one with China, that constrain the government of Canada from enacting any regulation that could impose unfavourable conditions on the investors or investor interests of the other countries.

These investment goals are also contained in APEC, the Asia Pacific Economic Cooperation forum, by far the boldest free trade initiative in the world. Made up of eighteen member "economies," including Canada (although APEC leaders use the term "economies" instead of "nation-states" in order to include the "three Chinas" — China, Hong Kong, and Taiwan — the term justifies the artificial separation of economic liberalization from social, environmental, and human rights issues), APEC is attempting to establish timetables to remove remaining nation-state barriers to trade and investment.

The sole criteria for membership is the desire to hasten the process of trade and investment liberalization in the region and to influence international trade organizations to this end. Says economist C. Fred Bergsten, former chairman of the APEC Eminent Persons Group, "Within the next two or three years, we should think in terms of holding the world's first global trade summit, drawing on the experience of the EU, of APEC, of the Miami Summit in the Western Hemisphere. We should put those programs together, through a global trade summit, and come to an objective of global free trade by 2010. APEC can be a major catalyst for that."

APEC leaders have declared that they will seek the explicit inclusion of the World Bank and the International Monetary Fund in the process in order to force nation-state compliance

agencies: OECD

APEC

through the granting or withholding of loans.

Yet, in spite of this proliferation of treaties and trade agreements granting ever-increasing protection to global investors, there are still loopholes, exemptions, overlaps, and limits by geographic region, sector, or issue that act as barriers to the complete supremacy of corporations. And national protectionist sentiment is still very strong in some parts of the world. This has only stiffened the resolve of corporations to create one universal, comprehensive, consistent, and binding investment treaty to settle the matter once and for all.

The Fall of Democratic Rights

The conclusion of the Uruguay Round of the GATT led to the creation in 1995 of the World Trade Organization, which monitors the movement of goods and capital across state borders and ensures state compliance with GATT rules. The central mandate of the WTO is to promote global free trade by working towards the elimination of all remaining tariff and non-tariff barriers to international investment and trade, and it contains no codes to protect the environment, labour rights, social programs, or cultural diversity. Laws passed by national or subnational governments (like Canadian provinces) can be directly challenged under the WTO by other member countries or their corporations on the grounds that they are "trade restrictive."

For instance, Canada and the United States successfully challenged a European ban on the importation of North American beef containing hormones Europe considered dangerous to human and animal health. It is the WTO that the U.S. magazine industry used to put a stop to the techniques Canada uses to ban split-run magazines. And Japan and the European Commission have come together to launch a WTO challenge against the state of Massachusetts for barring state agencies from buying goods or services from companies that do business in politically repressive Burma.

Once the final WTO ruling is made (by retired trade experts and unelected trade bureaucrats), worldwide conformity is required. A country is obligated to conform its laws to the WTO or face the prospect of perpetual trade sanctions. It is not surprising, therefore, that it is a central goal of the major powers to eventually lodge the MAI in the WTO, the most powerful international body the world has ever known. Says European Commission vice-president Leon Brittan, "On investment, the most important theme of all for the future of the world economy, we have at last put WTO on the map. Investment indeed seems to me THE top priority for WTO in the years ahead . . . It is also an issue which is primarily for the WTO because it involves the development of an appropriate framework of binding rules."

At the first WTO ministerial meeting in Singapore, in December 1996, the EU and Canada in particular pushed hard for agreement on making an investment treaty the centrepiece of future negotiations. But strong opposition from many developing countries slowed the process dramatically. Not only did they fear that such a treaty would strip them of their remaining sovereignty but they identified the treaty as a potentially new and virulent form of colonialism. The WTO compromised and set up a working group on trade and investment with a mandate to report back at the next ministerial meeting in 1998.

Meanwhile, the U.S. had been busy promoting another strategy. Its stated aim was to "obtain a high-standard multilateral investment agreement that will protect U.S. investors abroad." It had feared that if the WTO established the first terms of an MAI, they would be watered down. The U.S. preferred the liberalized investment-friendly venue of the OECD — the rich nations' club where the MAI was first conceived — to obtain a state-of-the-art agreement that would serve as the prototype to take back to the WTO. After all, with its member countries housing 477 of the Global Fortune 500 corporations, it is in the OECD's perceived self-interest to set corporate-friendly global rules.

The MAI being negotiated by the OECD is the most far-reaching investment-liberalization agreement ever written. The intention of the member countries is to ratify it at their meeting in the spring of 1998, and then to seek non-OECD signatories, as the MAI will have an accession clause similar to NAFTA's, allowing individual countries to sign on. This way, pressure will build within the WTO to bring the recalcitrant Third World nations on board. As the EU puts it, the protectionist practices of the developing world "should be outlawed." It delicately adds, "Since the dramatic change in East-West relations, it has become more evident that foreign investment is a scarce resource which no one can afford penalizing."

Andrew Jackson of the Canadian Labour Congress explains, "Put bluntly, if an MAI is concluded, it will be increasingly difficult for developing countries who want to attract foreign investment to remain outside. It is widely recognized that the central purpose of the MAI is to limit the role of the state in developing countries."

Meanwhile, the ascendency of the Washington Consensus over the UN Declaration is changing the face of the world. Within countries and between countries, the disparity between rich and poor is growing dramatically. In Canada, the disparity in the level of incomes between the top 20 percent and the bottom 20 percent is 7–1 and growing. In the U.S., it is 9–1 and growing. Worldwide, reports the United Nations, it is 150–1 and has doubled in the last thirty years. The richest 20 percent of the world's population now receives 83 percent of the world's income, while the poorest 60 percent receives just 5.6 percent of the income.

And so, the values of democracy and citizenship rights so eloquently put forward in the UN Declaration of Human Rights may come to an ignominious defeat on the Declaration's fiftieth anniversary. The United Nations itself has recently committed to establishing a framework for co-decision-making with the transnational corporate sector. This will happen, ironically, under the auspices of the Commission on Sustainable Development.

An early draft of the declaration arising from the ministerial meeting of the World Trade Organization contained a reference to the fact that all member signatories to the WTO were also signatories to the UN Declaration. The reference was soon removed. Perhaps the hypocrisy was just too much even for the hardened trade negotiators and politicians deciding the fate of the world. Canada's position on free trade and liberalized invest-ment, as well as our foreign policy in general, has taken a 180-degree turn. Canada was the sole hold-out to the original OECD investment codes and was a major stumbling block to U.S. attempts to introduce investment rules in the GATT talks of the early 1980s. Canada argued that any program of study proposed would be "unbalanced unless it were to address, at the same time, the behaviour of multinational corporations."

But Canada is now a leading proponent of the MAI and a champion of bilateral agreements that bind signatories to strict investment protection rules. During the preparatory talks for the Singapore WTO ministerial meeting, Third World nongovernmental organizations (NGOs) report, Canada threatened to boycott UNCTAD, a venue much more hospitable to the concerns of developing countries, if they succeeded in blocking the process to initiate an investment treaty at the WTO. Canada's APEC Individual Action Plan states, "Canada welcomes, and indeed actively seeks, foreign investment and has one of the world's most open and transparent investment regimes."

Says David Schneiderman of the Centre for Constitutional Studies at the University of Alberta, "Canada, which prides itself on having a foreign policy distinct and distanced from the United States, has emerged as a fervent advocate of U.S. trade policy."

TWO

THE EMERGENCE OF GLOBAL CORPORATE RULE

"This dispossession of citizens and communities of their
collective rights . . . is . . . grounded in a metaphysical principle:
that unfettered market rule has a natural right to regulate
all of the world's societies in their best interests."
— JOHN MCMURTRY, PROFESSOR OF PHILOSOPHY,
UNIVERSITY OF GUELPH

Opening the first ministerial
meeting of the World Trade Organization in December 1996,
WTO director general Renato Ruggerio declared that the drafting of a global investment treaty was like "writing the constitution of a single global economy." By this time, it had become
increasingly clear that the new WTO was largely designed to
advance the Washington Consensus and the corporate agenda of
the Trilateral Commission. After all, the central mandate of the
WTO is to liberalize trade and investment, giving transnational
corporations the freedom to move their investments and operations from one country to another, unfettered by government
intervention or regulation. But what does the drafting of a

Multilateral Agreement on Investment have to do with developing a constitution for the world economy? If an MAI is meant to be a global economic constitution, then what powers and tools does it give to transnational corporations as distinct from democratically elected governments? And what impact would all of this have on the democratic rights enshrined in the UN Declaration of Human Rights and related Covenants?

The prime objective of the MAI is to facilitate the movement of capital — both money and productive facilities — across international borders by setting rules to restrict countries from using legislation, policies, and programs to impede such movement. Thus any country that signs on to the MAI would be forbidden to require any transnational corporation to meet certain economic, social, environmental, or cultural standards considered important for the well-being of its citizens. These corporations could include petroleum companies like Shell Oil or Exxon, forestry conglomerates like Georgia-Pacific or Mitsubishi, auto giants like General Motors or Toyota, financial institutions like Citicorp or the Royal Bank of Canada, chemical enterprises like Bayer or DuPont, drug manufacturers like Pfizer or Bristol-Myers Squibb, agribusinesses like Cargill or Archer Daniels Midland, electronics companies like General Electric or Sony, telecommunications giants like AT&T or Northern Telecom, food manufacturers like Nestlé or RJR Nabisco, retail enterprises like Wal-Mart or K-Mart, food service companies like McDonald's or PepsiCo, or insurance conglomerates like Prudential or Nippon Life.

The MAI Toolbox

One way of looking at the MAI is to view it as a toolbox for corporations. As a body of investment rules, the various disciplines and mechanisms built into the MAI provide corporations with a set of power tools that can be used to challenge governments and restrict their ability to regulate the economy. The main source of energy used for these power tools is what is known in U.S. constitutional law as the "takings" rule. According to U.S. law, governments are prohibited from taking private property "without adequate compensation" and "valid public purpose." While the takings rule is meant to ensure fair treatment, it has much deeper implications when it becomes the core of trade and investment treaties.

The MAI, however, not only adopts the takings rule as the cornerstone of the treaty, but it also employs a broad definition of "investment" (property) and "expropriation" (taking), to the benefit of corporations. The agreement draws again on U.S. law when it comes to dispute resolution; in the U.S., disputes over property rights are settled through litigation in the courts. Although corporations in Canada can and do settle disputes through the courts, there has been a tradition in this country of using legislation and diplomatic processes to deal with these issues. Under the MAI, transnational corporations would be allowed to bring suits against governments in the domestic courts of their host countries as well as through international arbitration panels.

U.S. constitutional traditions have been applied before in the development of international trade and investment treaties. The core of NAFTA, and to some extent the WTO, is based on U.S. takings law and litigation procedures for resolving disputes. As the experience of NAFTA reveals, the takings rule has a hidden cost for citizens: while it is used to protect transnational corporations from any government intervention or regulation that inhibits the free flow of capital and profitable investment, it has the effect of "taking" away the power of governments to serve and protect the democratic rights of their citizens. There are no corresponding rules to protect governments from the takings of transnational corporations.

By using the MAI power tools, corporations will be able to take resources away from the public and the commons. These takings, some of which are outlined below, have a direct effect on the democratic rights of citizens and the democratic responsibilities of governments.

Take 1: Political Rights

The MAI contains provisions that, in effect, allow transnational corporations to assume political rights that were once the prerogative of nation-states. There is nothing particularly new about corporations having political rights. Throughout the twentieth century, corporations have been able to acquire a wide range of political rights under international law, as well as corporate law within countries. Indeed, corporations were granted legal rights to "personhood" and "citizenship" in most countries, including Canada, before either women or aboriginal peoples were. In the U.S., the Supreme Court even invoked the Fourteenth Amendment, which had initially been used for the protection of freed slaves, to grant corporations the same status as persons.

What is new in the MAI is the extent to which transnational corporations are granted the status of nation-states with political rights. Throughout the official draft text of the investment treaty, corporations are defined as investors with a legal status equal to that of the contracting parties to the agreement, namely, the member countries of the OECD. In other words, transnational corporations are to be treated as having a legal status equal to that of nation-states under the treaty. In some cases, it could be argued that the political rights to be conferred on corporations under the MAI even supersede those of nation-states. This becomes clearer when we look at the way the MAI's two basic operating principles — those of "most favoured nation" and "national treatment" — are applied.

In international trade agreements, when countries decide to grant most favoured nation status to another country, they agree to give that country the most favourable treatment they give to any trading partner. Under the MAI, this political privilege is also granted to corporations. That means a country like Canada must not only treat all the other twenty-eight member countries of the OECD, but also all transnational corporations based in those countries, as most favoured nations. All countries and their corporations are to be treated the same with respect to regulatory laws. According to the Preamble Center for Public Policy in Washington, D.C., this rule could prevent countries like Canada from applying economic sanctions against a member country by restricting Canadian corporations from doing business with it; nor could Ottawa deny market access to corporations from other member nations because of either their own or their home country's poor labour, environmental, or human rights records. The only exception here would be a United Nations plan for economic sanctions.

At the same time, transnational corporations would be accorded national treatment, requiring nations to treat foreign investors and their investments "no less favourably" than they treat their own domestic companies. The objective here is not only to eliminate discrimination against foreign-based corporations but also to ensure that they have both access to and presence in domestic markets. National treatment does not necessarily mean that governments cannot regulate; they simply must not discriminate against foreign corporations by favouring domestic firms. Under this rule, Canada could not, for example, place restrictions on what foreign investors can own (unless Ottawa obtained specific exemptions for its foreign ownership laws), nor could it maintain economic assistance programs that solely benefit domestic companies. While governments would be forbidden to discriminate against foreign investors, there would be nothing to stop them from treating foreign-based corporations more favourably than domestic ones. Even if a country imposed performance requirements on domestic companies, it could not apply them to foreign corporations.

In addition, the national treatment rule would apply to the appointment of senior management and boards of directors of transnational corporations. It would no longer be necessary for a foreign company operating in Canada, for example, to appoint a majority of Canadians to its board of directors. What's more, foreign-based corporations investing "a substantial amount of capital" would be assured that their key personnel (executives, managers, specialists) would be given free, unrestricted entry and authorization to work. In effect, domestic immigration and labour laws would be waived in favour of foreign-based corporations and their key personnel, thereby establishing a superior class of citizenship.

The MAI negotiators maintain that these measures are necessary to create what they call "equality of competitive opportunity." But they really amount to affirmative action for transnational corporations.

Take 2: Performance Standards

The MAI will take away the capacity of governments to require that foreign-based corporations meet performance standards in relation to key economic, social, and environmental objectives. At one time, Ottawa had a Foreign Investment Review Agency that required that transnational corporations meet certain performance standards before being allowed to proceed with their investment plans in Canada. Under NAFTA, Canada did obtain an exemption that allowed Ottawa to continue reviewing large-scale investments (i.e., investments of more than $150 million) and applied some limited performance requirements. At the same time, all foreign-based corporations are expected to follow Canada's business, tax, labour, and environmental codes.

Yet, the MAI is designed to go beyond NAFTA by establishing a more comprehensive ban on performance requirements issued by governments. Although NAFTA prohibits governments from requiring foreign companies to use domestic content (e.g., labour, resources, services), or transfer new technology, or export a certain level of manufactured goods, it does allow performance requirements for promoting economic development or addressing health, safety, and environmental standards. The MAI proposals, however, add to the list of restrictions: first, they will further limit performance requirements pertaining to the establishment, acquisition, expansion, or management of an investment (e.g., location of headquarters, employment levels, local hiring quotas, joint ventures, etc.); and second, they will limit a government's ability to attach performance requirements to subsidies or investment incentives (e.g., by banning export quotas and preferences for the purchase of domestic goods and services).

Although the MAI negotiators may not make the new investment rules (such as the rule of national treatment) applicable to government procurement programs, the proposed list of restrictions on performance requirements goes beyond the rules of NAFTA and the WTO, putting severe limits on what governments and public enterprises will be allowed to do in purchasing goods and services. Among the prohibited measures are any quotas on the export of goods and services, the sales of goods and services in the region, and the hiring of local personnel. Moreover, it is proposed that these bans on performance requirements be retroactive, which means that governments would be obligated to eliminate existing regulations and measures that do not conform with these new investment rules. And governments may not be allowed to enforce performance requirements previously negotiated with corporations that have received subsidies or investment incentives.

The MAI's ban on performance standards would go a long way towards providing investors with absolute protection. It even goes beyond national treatment. It is not simply concerned with standards that discriminate against foreign-based corporations. The ban means absolute prohibition.

To be sure, the OECD has adopted Guidelines for Multinational Enterprises, meant to promote labour, social, and environmental standards. These guidelines are to be attached to the official MAI text; however, they are purely voluntary for OECD member countries and their corporations. They would have no legal status and no binding effect on the interpretation of the investment rules. In short, it would appear that the inclusion of these guidelines for corporate behaviour is mainly for cosmetic purposes.

Meanwhile, the U.S. Council for International Business, the largest big-business lobby behind the MAI, has issued a stiff warning against attempts to negotiate any labour and environmental provisions, even weak sidebar agreements like those included in NAFTA. "The MAI is an agreement by governments to protect international investors and their investments and to liberalize investment regimes," said the USCIB president in a letter to U.S. officials on March 21, 1997. "We will oppose any and all measures to create or even imply binding obligations for governments or business related to environment or labor."

In effect, the MAI would confer rights and privileges on transnational corporations without any corresponding responsibilities and obligations to society, communities, or the common good.

Take 3: Public Enterprises

The MAI contains rules that take away the ability of governments to develop and promote public enterprises as engines of economic and social development. Here in Canada, crown corporations ranging from provincial electrical utilities to the Canadian Broadcasting Corporation (CBC), Canada Post, and the Wheat Board, along with our public education and health care systems, are examples of public enterprises that have co-existed with private enterprise in a mixed economy. While some of these public enterprises have traditionally held monopoly positions in the Canadian market, they have also had a corresponding social obligation to ensure that the goods and services they produced were equitably distributed to all citizens and all regions.

Although the MAI does not go so far as to call for the dismantling of public enterprises, it would compel them to act like private enterprise operations. Under the MAI, public enterprises will be required to act "solely in accordance with commercial considerations." This means that a crown corporation like Canada Post would end up charging exorbitantly high rates for postal services in the Northwest Territories, while rates in

Toronto would be, relatively speaking, much lower. All public enterprises would also have to adhere to the national treatment provisions in both their regulatory functions and their market operations. As a result, crown corporations would no longer be able to favour domestic producers over foreign companies when it comes to purchasing and/or selling goods and services or applying regulations in the marketplace.

In particular, the MAI seeks to eliminate "anti-competitive practices" by public enterprises. One such practice is called "cross-subsidization," whereby a crown corporation would provide economic support to local businesses by selling goods or services at below market rates. For example, hydro power and water utilities might provide discounted services to rural communities. The MAI, by restricting these practices, is seeking to give leverage to foreign-based companies trying to break into markets where public enterprises have traditionally held monopolies. Some OECD members have even proposed that public enterprises based on "national standards" be prohibited.

Even though the MAI proposals do not require governments to privatize their state enterprises, they do lay down a set of rules and disciplines to be followed once decisions have been made to privatize the ownership and control of public assets. The "national treatment" and "most favoured nation" clauses would go into effect immediately, being applied to the initial as well as subsequent stages of the privatization process. That means foreign-owned corporations as well as domestic companies would have to be informed at the same time and allowed to bid on the assets. Some OECD members have even proposed that governments be prohibited from utilizing "special share arrangements," under which local workers and/or communities would be encouraged to buy the company themselves.

Of course, many of these provisions were contained in NAFTA and Ottawa was successful in reserving its right to put limits on foreign purchases of shares when public assets were privatized, including limits on foreign ownership of Air Canada and Petro-Canada shares and other privatized crown corporations. But the MAI contains stronger language on these matters and there is no guarantee that Canada would be exempted from the application of these rules to future privatization endeavours. Moreover, it is expected that these MAI disciplines would apply to provincial as well as federal crown corporations, which was not the case with NAFTA. In any event, these measures are bound to radically alter the balance of power between public and private sectors of the economy over time.

Take 4: Political Clout

The MAI proposals give transnational corporations additional political clout by granting them the powers and mechanisms to sue governments directly. In other international trade agreements, only member states could sue other governments for damages. In the case of both NAFTA and the WTO, for example, dispute settlement mechanisms were established for governments to take action and resolve problems on a state-to-state basis. If a corporation had a dispute with the laws and programs of another country, it had to work through its own government to launch an action. While NAFTA allowed corporations to take legal action against member states on certain investment claims, the MAI would go much further.

Unlike NAFTA, the scope for litigation by corporations would include all disciplines of the MAI. Any breach of the MAI rules "which causes (or is likely to cause) loss or damage to the investor or his investment" would constitute grounds for legal action by corporations. This includes the rights of absentee landlords. For example, a British corporation could claim damages on behalf of its Canadian subsidiary if a loss of investment resulted from actions taken by Ottawa or a provincial government. It has even been proposed by MAI negotiators that "a lost opportunity to profit from a planned investment would be a type of loss sufficient to give an investor standing to bring an establishment dispute." In order to ensure that foreign corporations have the tools to enforce the terms of the agreement against governments, the MAI contains an investor-state dispute settlement mechanism.

This special mechanism provides investors or corporations with several options. Claims for damages could be filed against governments in either international tribunals or in domestic courts. The tribunals could take the form of arbitration panels like those set up under the WTO and NAFTA, or existing forums like the International Center for the Settlement of Investment Disputes in Washington, D.C. If challenged by a corporation, governments would be obligated to appear before the designated tribunal or court. Judgments would be based not on the laws of the host country but on the rules of the investment treaty itself. The arbitration panels, as well as the courts, would impose monetary awards for damages. All awards for damages would be "binding" and enforced "as if it were a final judgment of [the country's domestic] courts." Indeed, these legal mechanisms are designed to ensure that no government can deny enforcement of an award based on the claim that it would be "contrary to its public policy." In the past, the U.S. has strongly resisted giving this much power to the WTO arbitration panels, so it is not yet clear whether those provisions will be fully adopted.

If they are included in the treaty, these proposed mechanisms would provide transnational corporations with a powerful new weapon against governments and their regulatory policies. A concrete example is the $350 million lawsuit recently filed against Ottawa (under a special section of NAFTA) by the Ethyl Corporation, a U.S. chemical company, regarding Canada's ban on the import and transport of the gasoline additive MMT (see chapter four). Regardless of the outcome, the Ethyl suit will serve to demonstrate how these mechanisms are likely to be used by corporations to force governments into compliance with the new investment rules. Moreover, it is quite possible that a Canadian transnational corporation could make use of the same MAI tools to challenge Ottawa or the provinces, either by forming a joint venture with a foreign-based corporation to initiate a challenge, or perhaps by getting its own subsidiary in another country to take action.

At the same time, these mechanisms would not have to be fully exercised to have their desired effect. The fact that corporations would have these weapons at their disposal, coupled with the threat (implied or otherwise) to use them against governments, could generate considerable political clout. Indeed, it has been shown that various U.S. corporations have successfully used the NAFTA takings rule behind the scenes to subvert the Ontario government's plans for public automobile insurance, the federal government's proposals for the plain packaging of cigarettes, and the repudiation of contracts to privatize Terminal 2 of the Pearson International Airport in Toronto. There are likely dozens of lesser-known cases where corporations have used the threat of these tools to shape and determine government policy decisions. This is sometimes referred to as the "chill effect."

Take 5: Public Legislation

The MAI contains measures specifically designed to take away governments' ability to maintain existing laws or enact new laws in the public interest. Like most democratic societies, Canada has built up a vast body of economic, social, and environmental legislation designed to protect the public interest and the common good. This body of legislation covers a broad range of public concerns ranging from foreign ownership, consumer protection, and social programs to regional development, environmental conservation, and cultural identity. Yet, this kind of public interest legislation could very well be jeopardized by what the MAI proposes as "roll-back" and "standstill" clauses.

The roll-back clause is designed to ensure that any pieces of legislation or regulatory measures of member countries that did not conform with the basic principles and conditions of the MAI would be reduced and eventually eliminated. All member countries signing on to the agreement are expected to list in advance any current laws, policies, or programs considered "non-conforming" with respect to the disciplines of the MAI. This "hit list" could include laws restricting foreign ownership in strategic industries, banning large-scale water exports, preserving Canadian content in public broadcasting, or subsidizing Canadian cultural industries. Once governments sign on, they would make a commitment to establish a "sunset" process for any legislation that conflicted with the new investment regime.

To be sure, certain types of laws, policies, or programs might be exempted. For example, MAI negotiators have tentatively agreed to three general exemptions from their investor protections: national security, public order, and international peace and security. Any laws that did not fall into these categories would be subject to the MAI rules. There is some debate on the meaning of these terms and how broadly they can be defined. Canadian trade lawyer Barry Appleton claims that, in NAFTA, if the French term "*ordre public*" is used instead of the English term "public order," then the exemption could be widely defined. On the other hand, U.S. constitutional expert Robert Stumberg says the scope of these general exemptions is narrowly defined in the MAI, and therefore goes further than either the WTO or NAFTA in encroaching on the sovereign powers of nation-states.

Besides these general exemptions, governments would have the right to reserve or exempt more specific pieces of legislation. While these "country-specific reservations," as they are called, are necessary to win political support for the agreement in each country, the MAI negotiators have made it clear that there must be a commitment to limiting the life of these exemptions. They would be only temporary. If the Chrétien government, for example, petitioned to exempt pieces of its non-conforming social, cultural, and environmental legislation, it would be pressured to impose a "sunset" on such legislation over a period of time (say five or ten years). It is also clear that restrictions would be placed on the application of these country-specific reservations to ensure that they are not used by governments to avoid their basic obligations under the MAI.

At the same time, these roll-back measures would be reinforced by "standstill" provisions. These stipulate that governments not introduce any new non-conforming laws, policies, or programs in the future. In effect, the MAI would forbid any future government in Ottawa or the provinces to take public ownership or control over a sector of the economy that had been previously privatized or to reintroduce regulations that had been scrapped in the past. A freeze would be placed on public interest law-making authority in the future. The MAI negotiators explicitly state that the combination of "roll-back" and "standstill" is to have a "ratchet effect." "Any new liberalization measures," the draft agreement states, "would be 'locked in' so they could not be rescinded or nullified over time."

Take 6: Protective Measures

The MAI would contain provisions designed to take away the capacity of governments to protect their citizens and the public interest, calling upon the state to apply protective measures in favour of investors and the interests of transnational corporations. Under the MAI, no government would be allowed to "impair . . . the operation, management, maintenance, use, enjoyment or disposal of investments in its territory" by corporations based in another country. The role of governments, therefore, is twofold: to ensure that the properties of foreign-based corporations are protected and to provide a safe haven for profitable transnational investment.

In the MAI, investment protection is to be applied to virtually every stage of the investment cycle — pre-investment, operation, and management, plus the repatriation of profits and dividends. An investment, for the MAI's purposes, includes claims to money and performance, rights under contract, intellectual property rights, and real estate, as well as government concessions and licences. Investment protection under the MAI would encompass rights of access to natural resources and the right to contract to governments; it would also apply to speculative forms of investment, including the types of investment that contributed to the Mexican peso crisis. The scope for investment protection proposed by the MAI goes far beyond that of any other international agreement.

While all of the MAI mechanisms described so far have the effect of protecting foreign investments, one of the main defensive weapons in the MAI arsenal is the principle of no expropriation without adequate compensation. Indeed, there should be, say the drafters, "an absolute guarantee that an investor will be compensated for an expropriated investment." In using the term "expropriation," the MAI negotiators deliberately imply a broad definition of the term. They talk not only of expropriation, but also of "any other measure having a similar effect." This includes any government action that would "have the effect of depriving an investor of its investment," such as limits on the use and disposal of products and a variety of other regulatory measures that might have negative effects on the value of the investment.

Here, a prime objective of the negotiators is to ensure that the MAI "serves as a safeguard against new forms of expropriation in the future." This is why some negotiators have gone so far as to propose that certain corporate tax measures that do not conform with the basic principles and disciplines of the agreement could be designated as "creeping expropriation" for which corporations could demand compensation from governments. Furthermore, these protection measures against expropriation favour foreign corporations and investors over domestic companies. Even if a particular government regulation were applied equally to both domestic and foreign companies, foreign investors would still be able to claim compensation for any expropriation of their investment. Canadian investors, on the other hand, would not be able to use these MAI protection measures against the federal government, unless through a subsidiary in another country or a joint venture with a foreign-based corporation.

Another example of an investment protection measure is the MAI rule that all government incentives for investment be made subject to national treatment and therefore available to all foreign-based corporations. To promote local economic development, governments sometimes offer incentives ranging from subsidies to tax breaks. While domestic companies are often the intended beneficiaries of these incentives, foreign investors also want to be able to bid on them. National treatment would make that possible. Moreover, MAI negotiators object to the ways that government incentives are used to build the capacity of crown corporations or public enterprises to expand exports and compete globally. Not only does the MAI propose a stronger application of the national treatment rules to curb discrimination in the use of incentives, but an "effects test" might also be required to determine whether these government incentives cause injury to foreign corporations.

In the name of investment protection, governments would also be prohibited from restricting the operations of corporations from countries where there is widespread violation of human rights or environmental standards. The very fact that MAI negotiators have steadfastly refused to incorporate binding labour, environmental, and human rights obligations means that there is nothing in the treaty to permit governments to discriminate against corporations or countries that violate these standards. Furthermore, under the most favoured nations clause, governments would be prohibited from applying economic bans, sanctions, or embargoes to punish a member country with dismal human rights or environmental records by preventing its corporations from doing business. Such actions would be viewed as an interference with, and distortion of, the new investment rules and could be challenged under this clause as a violation of the MAI. The MAI would protect corporations from this kind of governmental action unless a direct connection with a violation of international laws can be proven.

Take 7: Public Revenues

The MAI also contains measures that would take away or greatly reduce the power of governments to generate public revenues from increased corporate investment. Governments traditionally rely on certain tools — such as an ability to tax corporate profits and control flows of capital outside the country — to regulate capital flows and generate income for public use. The agreement would seriously restrict their ability to use these tools.

The new investment regimen, for example, would include a ban on government restrictions on both the repatriation of profits and the movement of capital in general. Thus the Canadian government would no longer be able to require a foreign-based corporation to keep any of its Canadian-made profits in Canada. Even profits made on the sale of a local enterprise could be taken out of Canada and reinvested in the home country of the corporation or elsewhere. Nor could Ottawa or any of the provinces take legislative action to delay or prohibit a transnational corporation from moving out of the country any portion of its assets, including financial instruments like stocks or currency. A foreign-based corporation could not be prevented from taking a factory it just purchased and relocating it outside the country. By the same token, governments may not be able to require a forest company to process its timber before it is exported (even though Canada's right to ban the export of raw logs has been recognized under NAFTA).

This raises the question of what national governments could do to curb rampant speculation on financial markets. Every day, more than two trillion dollars' worth of currency is traded on money markets around the world via electronic networks. This traffic in "hot" money makes countries more vulnerable to external shocks like the "tequila effect" that destabilized financial markets in Mexico following the peso crisis in 1994. The experience of countries like Chile teaches us that nations that impose controls on the inflow and outflow of speculative capital are less vulnerable to these shocks. But the MAI's proposed ban on limits to the movement of capital would further tie the hands of national governments when it comes to controlling this particular kind of movement. There has been, however, some debate among MAI negotiators about whether an exception to this rule should be made in the case of an impending national financial crisis (like the Mexican peso collapse); this exception would allow governments to avoid financial meltdown by restricting investors from suddenly pulling tens of billions of dollars out of a particular country.

As we've seen, taxation measures that did not conform to the goals and disciplines of the MAI would be identified as instances of "creeping expropriation" for which corporations, in turn, could demand compensation from governments. The MAI negotiators have considered what other measures might be taken to curb the taxing powers of governments, although for the time being they have decided to exclude taxation from the MAI rules, pending further study. But the fact remains that they have begun to adopt a very broad view of taxation. Even payroll taxes and social security contributions are identified in the MAI's definition of taxation. If, in the future, the new investment rules were suddenly applied to taxation policy, the capacity of governments to raise public revenues for social programs in this country and elsewhere could be severely limited. In the meantime, the competitive climate for investment generated by the MAI would likely continue to put downward pressure on government taxation of corporations.

Take 8: Political Security

Finally, the MAI would compel governments to take on the obligation of guaranteeing a significant degree of political security for transnational corporations and their investments. One of the requirements of transnational corporations, when they are deciding where to invest, is the assurance of political stability and security. From the corporations' standpoint, it is the responsibility of the state to provide favourable conditions and a safe haven for profitable transnational investment and competition.

For these reasons, the MAI is designed to provide built-in measures guaranteeing a high degree of political security for corporations and their investments. Obviously, the roll-back and standstill clauses, reinforced by the rights of corporations to sue governments directly and by the investor-state dispute mechanism, are key to establishing such security. But perhaps the most "stabilizing" — and extraordinary — provision in the proposed agreement is the clause outlining the terms and conditions to which governments must conform if they decide to withdraw from the MAI.

In international trade agreements like NAFTA, participating governments are required to give six months' notice of their intention to withdraw from the agreement. Under the MAI, however, contracting governments would not be able to withdraw until five years after the agreement has come into force. On top of this, even if a future government decided to withdraw from the MAI, it is proposed that the rules would remain in effect for another fifteen years. In other words, once a country like Canada had ratified the agreement, it would be virtually locked in for a twenty-year period. Correspondingly, under this clause, all transnational corporations based in the contracting countries would have an ironclad guarantee that the new investment rules would remain in force for at least twenty years after the treaty had been ratified.

There are also provisions to ensure that this "high standard" investment treaty, as the U.S. negotiators call it, will be secured in the future, even if non-OECD member countries sign on to the agreement. One of the key terms of the accession clause, which stipulates the conditions of joining the MAI at a later date, would be the unconditional acceptance by new member countries of the investment rules ratified by the original OECD countries and their governments. Any amendments to the MAI proposed by new countries would have to be accepted and ratified by all the contracting governments in the agreement.

TOGETHER, THESE EIGHT "TAKINGS" constitute the core of the MAI. All eight are designed to favour transnational corporations by transferring resources and powers from the public to the private sector. For each of these takings, the MAI proposes a set of tools and mechanisms that function, in effect, to reorganize the role of the state or government to serve the interests of transnational corporations by promoting profitable investment and competition. And the driving force behind these takings, of course, would be in the power of corporations to sue governments directly. In short, transnational corporations would be able to use the power tools enshrined in the MAI to directly challenge and even dismantle unwanted government regulations.

It should be emphasized that these public takings could occur in two ways through the MAI: (1) by imposing legal and binding obligations on what governments can and cannot do; and (2) by creating an investment climate that constrains governments in creating policy. Even if the MAI rules did not compel governments to, for example, roll back specific pieces of social and environmental legislation, the MAI could certainly be used to create a "chill effect" that limits policy choices and forces governments to ratchet down their regulatory measures with regard to transnational corporations. If they have the political will, governments can, of course, resist these "chill effects," but not without considerable cost to the public.

As a result, this global investment treaty, which is going through the final drafting stages at the OECD in Paris, will go a long way towards advancing the Washington Consensus. Indeed, the MAI will, if it is ratified by the member OECD countries, effectively overrule and replace UN agreements like the Charter of Economic Rights and Duties of States. After all, it was this charter that gave nation-states the political authority to regulate foreign investment, by establishing performance standards for the operations of transnational corporations to ensure that national economic, social, and environmental priorities are served. Under the MAI, not only will nation-states be stripped of this political authority, but they will be compelled to use whatever authority they have to protect transnational investment and competition.

Perhaps this is what the WTO director general meant when he described the drafting of the investment treaty as "writing the constitution of a single global economy." When all is said and done, constitution-making has to do with codifying the rules of the game and the division of powers. Certainly, the new investment rules will radically alter the balance of power — between transnational corporations and democratically elected governments, between the private sector and the public sector, between investors and citizens — in the global economy. Moreover, given the fact that these investment rules and disciplines are binding, they will put enormous constraints on the democratic decision-making processes of governments and the range of public policy choices available to them. Political scientist Stephen Gill calls this global rule-making process by corporations and governments the "new constitutionalism," which has been taking shape through the negotiation of trade and investment treaties since the collapse of the Berlin Wall.

This new global constitution-making has been going on in secret, behind closed doors, with no public consultation whatsoever. And the crafters of this constitution are not elected officials. On the contrary, the MAI has largely been patched together by senior government and business bureaucrats. In the U.S., for example, the thirty-six advisory committees on trade and investment policy issues in Washington are dominated by more than 500 representatives of big business. The U.S. Council for International Business, which has been the driving force behind the MAI, claims to participate in regular meetings with the negotiators "immediately before and after each MAI negotiating session." Senior executives of U.S. transnationals like AT&T and IBM are known to be playing a key role in the negotiating process.

What is emerging through the OECD negotiations, therefore, is not simply an international investment treaty. It is really a global constitution for corporate rule. After all, almost all of the Global Fortune 500 companies are based in OECD member countries: 153 are U.S. corporations, 141 Japanese, 42 French, 40 German, 32 British, 16 Swiss, 12 Italian, 11 Dutch, 6 Canadian, 6 Belgian, 6

Spanish, 4 Australian, 3 Swedish, 2 Norwegian, 2 Finnish, and 1 Mexican. Indeed, it would seem that the MAI is being developed to give the Fortune 500 the powers and tools they need to rule the world through their own nation-states and contracting governments. If the MAI is ratified and then expanded through the accession clause to include non-OECD countries, particularly those from Asia and Latin America, it will sooner or later be incorporated as the driving force behind the WTO, arguably the dominant institution of global governance in the new world order. Should this happen, the MAI would be enshrined as the constitutional cornerstone of global corporate rule.

THREE

THE ASSAULT ON ECONOMIC RIGHTS

"The essence of independence is the reconstruction of the local economy, development of local enterprises, and retaining as much of the income and value-added in the domestic economy. The MAI is designed to erode significantly this right of national governments."

— MARTIN KHOR, THIRD WORLD NETWORK

Throughout the twentieth century, working people in Canada and other democratic societies have struggled to gain recognition of their fundamental economic rights as citizens. Basic to these rights has been the goal of full employment — the right of every citizen to a decent job. After all, it is through employment that people are able to gain an income to meet their basic living needs, achieve a sense of self-worth and human dignity, and participate in the progress of society. It has been commonly understood that a society espousing full employment and fair wages will foster a positive economic climate, as people feel secure enough to buy and invest.

It has also been recognized that to create such economic conditions, full employment must be buttressed by other economic rights. These include the right to fair wages and social benefits, unemployment insurance as a safety valve for economic downturns, the maintenance of health and safety standards in the workplace, and equal pay for work of equal value. In order to ensure that these and related economic rights are upheld, working people have the right to associate and form labour unions and the right to negotiate collective agreements with their employers that have a binding effect for the duration of the contract. These economic rights were made universal through the UN Declaration and its Covenants and the conventions of the International Labour Organization.

It was the nation-state, however, that became the chief agency responsible for seeing that these economic rights were implemented and enforced. Over the past sixty years or so, it has generally been understood that governments have the right and the responsibility to intervene in the marketplace for the purpose of defending and protecting the economic rights of their citizens, especially during downturns in the business cycle. In most democratic societies, laws were passed to facilitate union organizing, protect labour standards, establish unemployment insurance, ensure a minimum wage, stimulate employment equity, provide consumer protection, regulate foreign ownership, and enhance regional economic development.

Canada was no exception. Following the Great Depression, the role and responsibilities of the Canadian state were reorganized to promote economic rights. In the late 1930s, for example, the National Employment Commission insisted that employment was a national responsibility and urged government intervention in the economy to create jobs, especially in times of high unemployment. In 1940, the Rowell Sirois Report established the authority of the federal government over the national economy and laid the foundation for Ottawa's involvement in economic planning and development. Through the 1944 White Paper on Employment and Income, Ottawa made full employment a national priority.

Before, during, and after World War II, the federal government became increasingly involved in economic planning and development. As top priority was given to job creation, the Bank of Canada maintained a policy of low interest rates to promote full employment. The Canadian Wheat Board was set up in 1935 to ensure fair prices for farmers in the export of their wheat. The provinces established labour codes and minimum wage laws. Ottawa expanded its unemployment insurance program and introduced consumer protection legislation.

By the 1960s, however, it was evident that the federal government and the provinces could not maintain their commitment to full employment as long as the Canadian economy was dominated by foreign-owned corporations.

External Threats

As U.S. investment in Canada's resource and manufacturing industries continued to rise, Canadians began to see an increasingly large proportion of the nation's wealth leaving the country to line the pockets of foreign investors. Eventually, the Foreign Investment Review Agency was set up to regulate the buyouts and operations of foreign-owned corporations in the Canadian economy. Petro-Canada and the National Energy Program were put in place to assert more Canadian control over the country's energy and natural resources. In addition, the Department of Regional

Economic Expansion, along with the Canada Development Corporation, were initiated to promote economic development throughout the country.

By the 1980s, all of these initiatives were seen as obstacles to the Trilateral Commission's agenda and the Washington Consensus. Under the umbrella of the Business Council on National Issues, the 150 largest corporations in Canada launched a series of campaigns demanding an end to government intervention and regulation of the economy as well as a series of fire sales of crown corporations and public enterprises. Once the two free trade deals, the FTA and NAFTA, were firmly in place, most of the federal government agencies and programs that had been set up to promote, in part at least, the economic rights of Canadians, had either been severely weakened or dismantled altogether. Now the MAI and its corporate toolbox for public takings threaten to greatly accelerate the dismantling of our economic rights as citizens, in a number of areas.

Economic Planning

Despite repeated election promises of jobs! jobs! jobs! the Chrétien government in Ottawa has taken no action to launch a national employment strategy since taking office in late 1993. Instead, it has relied on the private sector, both Canadian and foreign-owned corporations, to create the country's much needed jobs and reduce the high levels of unemployment. Ottawa's abandonment of the task of direct job creation is not entirely surprising, since the government surrendered many of its powers and tools for economic planning through the new free trade regimes like NAFTA and the WTO. If the proposed MAI comes into effect, Ottawa and the provinces will be severely restricted in their efforts to develop any meaningful national economic plan or comprehensive employment strategy.

Under the MAI, federal and provincial governments would no longer be able to require that foreign-owned corporations investing in Canada create a certain number of jobs for Canadians in exchange for access to our resources and markets. Nor could Ottawa or the provinces require foreign investors to use certain kinds of job-preserving technologies in their plants or to balance imports with a certain level of exports in order to maintain jobs. There are even proposals in the draft MAI prohibiting governments from requiring foreign corporations to do a specific amount of research and development, train workers and provide services, construct or expand facilities, or locate a certain level of production in their countries. All of these activities constitute performance standards and requirements for foreign investors, requirements that could be ruled out of order under the MAI. While the WTO and NAFTA also prohibit governments from applying various kinds of performance standards, unlike the MAI, they do include a number of general exemptions to these rules. What's more, in the MAI these prohibitions would be applicable to all levels of government.

One of the principal tools used by all Canadian governments — federal, provincial, municipal — has been local procurement programs. Through such programs, governments are able to directly stimulate local job creation by using public revenues to purchase goods and services from local industries or businesses. Government procurement programs are frequently used to promote the economic development of particular constituencies like aboriginal peoples or women. Under the MAI rules, these practices could be viewed as discriminating against foreign-based companies or as creating market distortions that hinder private investment. While the WTO does have an Agreement on Government Procurement, there are a number of general exceptions where the obligations of the agreement do not apply. The same is likely to hold true for the MAI. Rules like national treatment are not expected to be applied directly to government procurement programs. But, as we have seen, the MAI outlines new restrictions on performance require-ments (ranging from local hiring to the purchase of domestic goods and services) that directly affect the procurement programs of governments and public enterprises. Moreover, the rights of corporations to sue governments, combined with the investor-state dispute settlement mechanisms, mean that the MAI rules could have a more powerful effect than any WTO agreement.

At the same time, attempts by Ottawa and the provinces to stimulate new job creation through the use of tax incentives are more than likely to be thwarted if the MAI proposals are adopted. Many provincial governments, for example, have used tax incentives as a policy tool to entice corporations to create a specified number of new jobs or locate their investment in a certain region. Similarly, tax incentives have been used to enhance the competitive position of federal and provincial crown corporations. The WTO already bans the discriminatory use of tax measures, but the MAI proposals give more ammuni-tion to foreign-based corporations to challenge outright any use of tax incentives by governments to influence the operations of particular corporations or to favour the competitiveness of local businesses and public enterprises. The same goes for governments' use of non-tax incentives, such as business subsi-dies, low interest loans, customized job training, or equity investments. In the end, governments would be left with a great deal more "carrots" (investment incentives) than "sticks" (regu-lating tools).

In effect, the MAI would hinder governments from playing a direct role in building the cornerstone of economic rights, namely, full employment. The recent Jobs and Timber Accord negotiated by the British Columbia government to create 22,000 new jobs in the forest industry over the next four years (plus another 17,000 spin-off jobs) could be directly challenged by foreign-based corporations under the MAI. As Premier Glen Clark put it, the accord is based on the principle that "access to public timber is a privilege that should be tied to the delivery of jobs and other social benefits." To ensure that this happens, the Clark government is using "a combination of incentives and compliance measures," say B.C. forestry officials. Companies that fail to meet their job targets "will be subject to sanctions which may include loss of access to innovative forest practices agreements and Forest Renewal B.C. funding." Such sanctions would not be tolerated if the MAI's proposed ban on performance requirements were in place today.

Although the Chrétien government might try to protect the right to make use of these kinds of policy tools to stimulate job creation through some kind of special reservation for Canada, it is questionable whether Ottawa would be granted such an exemption unless it were also given to all the other OECD countries. Even if Canada were to obtain such an exemption, how long would it last, given the MAI demand that governments roll back "non-conforming practices"?

Corporate Jobs

In a global economy dominated by the proposed MAI rules, governments would no longer have the policy tools and instruments necessary to create societies based on full employment.

Instead, the role of government would be to create a favourable and secure climate for transnational investment. Corporations, then, would supposedly create jobs, in response to the market forces of supply and demand. Essentially, this is the message that the Business Council on National Issues delivered to the Chrétien government following the 1997 federal election. The BCNI warned that any surplus in public revenues resulting from the recent battle waged against the deficit through massive cuts in government spending must not be used by Ottawa for direct job creation. What the federal government must do is support the business community. The jobs will come.

Indeed, Ottawa has more or less been pursuing this economic strategy since the early 1980s, with highly questionable results. Both federal and provincial governments have bent over backwards to accommodate the demands of big business — whether by deregulating the economy, privatizing public enterprises, fighting inflation, implementing free trade, slashing social spending, or downsizing the public sector. Yet, Canadians still suffer from chronic high unemployment. In March 1996, in its Throne Speech, the Chrétien government called on big business to play its role in dealing with "the human deficit of unemployment." Two days later, Industry minister John Manley appeared before a gathering of business leaders at the Empire Club in Toronto and sheepishly asked, "What are we going to do about the fact that corporations are making record profits and laying off people in droves?"

Despite raking in a record $66 billion in profits in 1995, Canada's leading corporations were laying off thousands of workers. General Motors eliminated 2,500 jobs while breaking the national record for corporate profits ($1.39 billion). The Canadian Imperial Bank of Commerce increased its profit margins by more than a billion dollars, yet laid off 1,290 employees. Canadian Pacific boosted its profits by 75 percent but laid off 1,500 workers. And Bell Canada took in half a billion dollars in profits while cutting 3,100 people from its payroll. Meanwhile, the compensation packages paid to the CEOs of these corporations skyrocketed.

Although Canada's economy began to show signs of growth midway through 1997, corporate downsizing trends continued. Bell Canada, for example, announced it was letting go another 2,200 workers, with more layoffs still to come. Since 1995, Bell has eliminated 15,200 jobs while creating only 2,000 new jobs.

The Chrétien government's job plan is largely based on substantially increasing Canada's trade in world markets. For every billion dollars in exports, officials frequently claim, another 15,000 jobs are created. But this is largely a myth, concludes David Ranney of the University of Illinois, after studying the job-creating performance of five major exporting U.S. corporations under free trade. Job claims based on export gains, says Ranney, ignore the negative impacts on jobs that result from rising imports. While Canada's exports have risen sharply under NAFTA, so too have our imports. In turn, this trend has had a particularly negative impact on Canadian manufacturers who produce primarily for our domestic market. According to the Alliance of Manufacturers and Exporters Canada, the portion of domestic sales of manufactured goods generated from Canadian-made products plummeted from 73 percent in 1980 to 40 percent in 1996. The remaining 60 percent of the market was made up by the import of manufactured goods from other countries. When manufacturers lose their market share to foreign industries, there is a corresponding drop in employment for Canadians.

Meanwhile, a number of the employment-related government programs highlighted in the Chrétien government's Red Book II could be targeted under the proposed MAI rules as government subsidies or incentives subject to national treatment. They include the Program for Export Market Development (which pays for half the costs of international market promotion for small and medium-sized businesses); the Canada Foundation for Innovation (which supports research infrastructure development in universities and hospitals); Technology Partnerships Canada (which provides capital for pre-commercial innovation); the Industrial Research Assistance Program (which financially assists more than 3,000 companies annually in research and development projects); small business loans (which provide up to $14 billion in loans to small Canadian companies); the proposed Transitional Jobs Fund (which is meant to create 15,000 jobs in high unemployment regions); the proposed $400 million grants to aboriginal-owned ventures; plus various farm support programs like the Agri-Food Credit Facility (which aids farm exports). At the very least, under the MAI's national treatment clause, these government subsidies and incentives would have to be made available to foreign-owned corporations as well as Canadian-based companies.

Foreign Investment

The prime objective of the MAI, of course, is to promote and facilitate transnational investment. Perhaps more than most countries, Canada's economy has been highly dependent upon foreign investment. The question for us is whether foreign investment, as it becomes less constrained by government intervention and regulation, serves to advance or hinder people's economic rights. To what extent is increased foreign investment essential for the creation of new jobs? What kinds of jobs are generated by foreign investment? What wage levels and working conditions can be expected from foreign-based corporations? And what kinds of obstacles to people's economic rights are generated when governments are no longer able to put conditions on foreign investors? These are the questions that emerged when, for example, Nike, the giant footwear corporation, took over a plant in Cambridge, Ontario, in 1994 to produce the world-famous Bauer hockey skates. Nike is a multi-billion-dollar marketing enterprise that usually contracts its manufacturing out to Asian factories where wages are low and unions are rare. Nike's takeover of the Bauer plant was trumpeted as a golden opportunity for the Montreal-based company. But in the spring of 1997, Nike announced it was shutting down the Bauer plant in Cambridge, throwing 400 unionized workers out of their jobs. Besides the legendary Bauer name, it appears that all Nike ever wanted from the Cambridge takeover was access to the Canadian company's technical expertise so that it could train its Asian workers how to make hockey skates.

Obviously, the Nike takeover of the Bauer plant was not closely scrutinized and monitored by either Ottawa or Queen's Park. No performance requirements were established to protect the Bauer product or the workers. Indeed, Ottawa has done little to demand that foreign-based corporations adhere to specific performance standards in the takeover of Canadian companies, especially since the Mulroney government replaced the Foreign Investment Review Agency with Investment Canada in 1985. Instead of reviewing and monitoring foreign takeovers, Investment Canada was given a mandate to solicit and promote foreign direct investment in Canada. Today, even Investment Canada no longer exists as a separate government agency. Under the Chrétien government, its functions have been absorbed into the Department of Industry, which, in turn, has become the main cheerleader for foreign investment.

Yet, even if Ottawa had wanted to apply specific performance requirements in the Nike takeover case, it would have been constrained in doing so by NAFTA. Although Canada has reserved its right under NAFTA to review foreign investment takeovers amounting to more than $150 million, the investment code makes performance requirements difficult to apply and enforce. The MAI rules would further tie Ottawa's hands. For example, not only would it be impossible to require that Nike adopt certain measures and conditions designed to protect the Bauer product and the workers' jobs in the Cambridge plant, but Ottawa would not even be able to require that the technology and expertise developed in Canada be kept here, let alone that a percentage of the profits made be retained in this country rather than siphoned off by the Nike headquarters in Beaverton, Oregon.

What's more, it can be argued that the type and impact of foreign direct investment have changed considerably in a climate of deregulated trade and investment. The new free trade regime has not, as promised, resulted in more job-creating forms of U.S. investment. From 1988 through 1994, Canadians invested $10.6 billion more in the United States than U.S. investors brought to Canada. Some 93 percent of all foreign investment in Canada between 1989 and 1991 was used to acquire existing Canadian firms rather than establish new businesses. Not only do acquisitions like this mean no new jobs are created, but they frequently result in layoffs as new owners attempt to streamline their operations. In addition, as finance analyst John Dillon notes, "More and more foreign investment in Canada is going to speculative purchases of government bonds and minority shares in enterprises instead of into new production that would create jobs."

Labour Standards

One of the key instruments used by democratically elected governments to defend and promote the economic rights of workers is labour legislation. In Canada, provincial governments have been primarily responsible for developing their own labour codes. To greater or lesser degrees, these provincial labour codes have protected the rights of workers by establishing basic standards and rules for the formation of unions, collective bargaining practices, collective agreements, workplace health and safety, and the conduct of a strike vote. While it is doubtful whether foreign-based corporations would try to use the MAI rules to strike down provincial labour codes directly, the new investment treaty would most certainly create a more competitive climate, which would put additional pressure on governments to weaken parts of their labour codes.

In both Ontario and British Columbia, for instance, the battle lines have already been drawn in the struggle over the future of provincial labour codes. On the one hand, the Harris government in Ontario has proposed legislation to amend the province's labour code to (among other things) restrict collective bargaining practices in the public sector. On the other hand, the Clark government in British Columbia initially brought forward legislation designed to (among other things) make it easier for workers to organize unions (e.g., in the construction sector), but then withdrew it because of mounting protests from the business community. These examples show that this kind of economic rights legislation is increasingly the target of attack by big business in this country. Labour laws are viewed as obstacles to investment by both domestic and foreign-based corporations. By greatly increasing capital mobility, the MAI would accelerate competitive pressures and exacerbate the bidding wars between provincial governments for foreign investment. The result would be a weakening of labour codes and standards.

At first glance, employment equity laws appear to be more directly vulnerable under the proposed MAI rules. In order to remedy economic inequality between groups of citizens, laws have been established by all levels of government to promote the hiring of aboriginal peoples, women, and disabled persons. The proposed MAI ban on performance requirements would have been sufficient to strike down such laws, but a recent amendment to the MAI draft text indicates that employment equity regulations would be acceptable. Even so, this amendment remains open to interpretation, and corporations may see fit to challenge policies like the Northwest Territories' requirement that northern and aboriginal peoples make up a certain percentage of workers in major resource development projects.

Canada's responsibility to promote labour rights in countries with repressive regimes would also be highly restricted under the MAI. In the past, Canadian governments have sometimes shown leadership by resisting the repression of labour rights in countries that employ tactics such as the imprisonment of labour leaders, the crushing of worker unrest, the outlawing of labour strikes, and the exploitation of child labour. Under the MAI, the use of sanctions on trade and investment, which were important tactical tools in the dismantling of apartheid in South Africa, could well be challenged by transnational corporations and banks. And Ottawa may not be able to introduce legislation compelling Canadian mining companies, for example, to apply our own labour laws or the conventions of the International Labour Organization in their Asian operations.

In particular, the proposed MAI clause on "secondary investment boycotts" could prove to be a major obstacle for Canada in promoting labour rights internationally. To be sure, the Helms-Burton legislation in the U.S., which attempted to bar Canadian companies doing business in Cuba from entering the United States, would be viewed as a direct violation of the secondary boycott clause in the MAI. Yet, the same clause could be used to stop any measures taken by Ottawa to ban imports by U.S., Japanese, British, or French corporations of products made by child labour in Burma or Indonesia.

Wage Disparities

Every province in Canada has passed a law establishing a minimum hourly wage, below which no company or business can legally pay its workers. While this minimum wage varies greatly from province to province and, in most cases, the rate falls below the poverty line, the legislation does at least protect workers' economic rights by setting a legal lower limit. Once again, there is nothing in the MAI rules to say that minimum wage laws must be eliminated. As long as they are applied equally to Canadian and foreign-based corporations, minimum wage laws could remain on the books. In the context of globalization, however, the MAI would intensify competitive pressures to lower or even eliminate minimum wage rates as an impediment to investment.

Over the past two decades, the minimum wage rate has certainly been slipping in comparison to the poverty lines in this country. According to the National Council on Welfare, the minimum wage in 1976 in all provinces except Ontario provided an income that was above the poverty line. The rate set by Saskatchewan, for example, provided an income that was 118 percent of the poverty line, while the rate in Prince Edward Island was 103 percent. By 1994, all the provincial minimum wage rates had dropped well below the poverty line, ranging from 67 percent to a high of 89 percent of the poverty line. Indeed, the federal minimum wage rate is even lower, at 53 percent. In short, people earning the minimum wage rate in this country today are already legally consigned to a life of poverty.

The MAI, however, would provide foreign-owned corporations with the tools to put downward pressure on minimum wage laws and rates. It is possible that a foreign-based corporation, spurred on by its subsidiaries and small business allies, could use the MAI rules to challenge a province that substantially raises its minimum wage rates, claiming that such policies impose performance requirements that constitute a form of expropriation. While such a move may seem to have a limited chance of success, its threat could likely generate a "chill effect."

Meanwhile, says Andrew Jackson of the Canadian Labour Congress, real wage levels, while barely keeping pace with the cost of living over the past fifteen years, have fallen way behind the earnings of company bosses. In 1995, for example, Frank Stronach's compensation package as chief executive officer at Magna International was 1,100 times the average wage earned by Magna workers that year. At the same time, Gerald Pencer's pay package at the Cott Corporation was 927 times that of the company's average employee; Paul Desmarais's package at Power Corporation was 249 times the average paid to his workers; Richard Thomson's at Toronto Dominion Bank was 230 times that of his tellers; Edgar Bronfman's was 180 times that of the average worker at Seagram; and Crawford Purdy at Imasco received a pay package that was 100 times that of his plant workers.

With pressure from Canadians, Ottawa could someday decide to bring in legislation to narrow the gap between the pay packages given to the CEOs of giant corporations and the wages paid to their employees. While there may be no specific rules in the MAI to prevent Ottawa from doing so, some foreign-based corporations (and Canadian companies as well) could claim such legislation was inconsistent with the investment treaty and use whatever MAI disciplines they could to invoke the standstill clause.

Regional Development

Overcoming regional inequalities has traditionally been a major priority in the pursuit of economic rights in Canada. To facilitate a sharing of national wealth, a system of equalization payments from rich to poorer provinces has become one of the hallmarks of the Canadian federation. But many of the policy efforts used by Ottawa and the provinces to promote greater regional economic development and equality have either become, or are in the process of being, phased out. Ottawa's Department of Regional Economic Expansion, which was designed to attract investment and stimulate development in the poorer regions of the country, has been abandoned. As we have seen, the proposed MAI would impose major restrictions on the use of performance requirements to support and strengthen local economic development, to the detriment of the territories and the Atlantic provinces.

Increasingly, provincial governments in the Atlantic region have been using limited public revenues to create lucrative tax and training incentives meant to attract foreign investors. In 1994 the McKenna government in New Brunswick used generous training grants to entice United Parcel Service to relocate its operations and 900 jobs from British Columbia. More recently, the new MacLellan government in Nova Scotia used similar tactics to get the U.S. communications giant, AT&T, to set up a telephone call centre — and one thousand jobs — in Halifax.

While new job creation is a welcome sight in these provinces, their governments are compelled to pay a hefty price for these investments with no ability to apply performance standards such as decent wages. This establishes a "beggar thy neighbour" policy for regional development, which allows footloose corporations to engage in bidding wars with provincial governments for scarce public revenues. Moreover, the MAI rules of national treatment for government investment incentives would greatly intensify this approach to regional development in the future.

The MAI restrictions on governments promoting regional economic development and equality would go even further. The MAI negotiators have decided, for example, to apply the agreement's investment rules to financial services. This means that any current or future laws requiring commercial banks to invest a portion of their holdings in local communities, particularly economically deprived areas, would likely be challenged as imposing a performance requirement on investors. Moreover, the MAI rules will likely reinforce the proposed WTO Financial Services Agreement due to be completed at the end of 1997. Under these new financial service obligations, Ottawa would have to open up Canada's market to foreign-owned banks. This would compel our nationally chartered banks to operate more like global financial giants that care less and less about local consumer and economic development needs while using the deposits of Canadians to finance megaprojects abroad and maximize their profits. Furthermore, regional development plans would be adversely affected by the fact that real estate is included in the MAI's broad definition of investment. Laws restricting the foreign ownership of land in P.E.I., for example, could eventually be struck down if challenged under the MAI, even if Ottawa obtains a temporary reservation.

At least one type of regional development strategy would be acceptable under the MAI. It involves what are often called "free trade zones" or "export processing zones." These are designated economic areas where transnational corporations are permitted to manufacture, process, and export goods duty-free. There are now 500 such zones worldwide, most of them located in Asian and Latin American countries. Each zone forms an enclave, sealed off from the rest of the economy and society by high fences, and usually patrolled by private security forces. Within these economic zones, corporations are allowed to operate outside the labour and environmental laws of the host country. Desperate to attract investment and jobs, the host governments willingly abdicate responsibility for the workers and openly suspend national labour and environmental laws. In such zones, child labour is rampant and deaths due to toxic waste and chemical and gas poisoning are common.

In Mexico and Central America, these free trade zones are called *maquiladoras*, and they have been a bonanza for transnational companies. The workers in their plants are young, docile, and largely female. The corporations operating in these zones are not required to pay income or property taxes to the host country, let alone customs duties on the export of their products. Usually, all of their profits can be taken out of the host country without any penalties. The companies are neither required to transfer their technology nor contribute to the industrial development of the host country. At the same time, union organizing is either severely restricted or banned outright. In El Salvador, for example, the government issues "certificates of good conduct" to identify anti-union job applicants and circulates the names of union organizers to ensure that they will never be hired again.

Some will say that this could never happen in Canada. But,

due to a little-known change in federal legislation, municipalities can now form a free trade or export processing zone without federal government sanction. Recently a Toronto-based developer announced plans to establish the first free trade zone for transnational corporations in Canada, to be located on the outskirts of Saint John, New Brunswick. While it may be designed as a kinder, gentler version of the *maquiladoras*, this free trade zone could become a prototype for the "regional development" acceptable under the MAI's investment rules.

IN SO MANY WAYS, if passed, the MAI will compromise the economic rights of Canadians, by constraining governments' ability to intervene in the marketplace when it is necessary to defend the rights of their citizens. While the majority of Canadians will suffer, the hardest hit are likely to be women, youth, and children. According to a recent study on jobs and women in the OECD countries, 23.7 percent of Canadian workers are in low-paid full-time work, second only to the United States, where the figure is 25 percent. At the same time, the percentage of working Canadian women involved in low-paid employment is 34.3 percent, second only to Japan (37.3 percent), and even higher than in the U.S. (32.5 percent). Indeed, the proliferation of low-paid, part-time employment is driving women, along with their children and the youth of this country, further into poverty.

Although its proponents would deny it, with the MAI on the horizon, economic conditions for average citizens will likely get worse. And erosion of economic rights affects more than basic living conditions; after all, citizens can hardly be expected to participate in their communities and the democratic process if they are denied decent paying jobs and working conditions. What does this say about the future of democracy?

FOUR

THE THREAT TO ENVIRONMENTAL RIGHTS

"If an animal goes extinct that is not economically useful,
no human is going to care too much."
— JIM SHEEHAN, COMPETITIVE ENTERPRISE INSTITUTE, WASHINGTON

The earth is in crisis. Large-scale resource extraction, from forests to fisheries, combined with the misuse of the world's land, air, and waterways, has created a global environmental emergency in which between 150 and 200 species of plants and animals become extinct every twenty-four hours. Elizabeth Dowdeswell of the UN Environment Program calls this a "mass annihilation caused by humankind's unsustainable methods of production and consumption" and adds, "With so much being lost, it's an open question whether the human species can survive."

Nations everywhere are giving their resource heritage to transnational corporations who extract it for profit and move on, leaving in their wake stripped forests, flooded lands, gaping mine holes, dirty air, and fouled water. The World Watch Institute predicts that ecological deterioration and environmental degradation will eclipse ideological conflict as the world's dominant national security concern in the coming years. And at precisely the wrong moment in history, the MAI is coming into play, to dramatically undermine any nation-state and international efforts to counteract this global threat.

Canada's Environmental Heritage

Every Canadian knows that we have inherited a land of wondrous bounty. No other nation on earth can boast such an abundance of forests, minerals, great lakes and rivers, fish, wildlife, prime farmland, and wild spaces. Canada's history and its legacy spring from and have been shaped by this great heritage.

Canada's policy on the protection of its environment and natural resources has been mixed; on some issues, it is non-existent. We have yet to pass even the most basic federal legislation to protect endangered species or their habitats. We have allowed wanton clear-cutting of our forests, overfishing of our oceans, and unbridled corporate mining and energy exploration.

Nevertheless, the federal government oversees a national parks system, forestry and freshwater research, protection of fisheries and ocean marine animals, the registration of toxic chemicals and pesticides, and environmental assessment procedures for projects with a federal role. It also represents Canada in international environmental talks and accords on issues ranging from climate change and acid rain to cleanup of the Great Lakes.

Canada became the first industrialized country to sign and ratify the Biodiversity Convention, committing us to protect species and habitat; Canada also signed the Framework Convention on Climate Change, the goal of which was to stabilize greenhouse gas emissions and reduce carbon dioxide emissions. And Canada was also a full and proud participant in the 1992 UN Earth Summit in Rio, taking a leadership role in assuring the full participation of NGOs in the process.

Provincial governments also have mixed environmental records. Some have passed their own endangered species protection laws, but enforcement has been uneven. All have set up provincial parks, with a sliding scale of standard enforcement. Most have created wilderness, wetland, or coastal protection areas and recycling programs, all of which are limited at best.

Provinces are responsible for many aspects of the regulation of forestry, mining and fishing, land-use planning, industrial waste monitoring and standard enforcement, and energy management and conservation. There are some notable examples of success. British Columbia restricted urban sprawl under farmland protection regulations; Ontario's stellar Conservation Authorities once set a world standard in protecting the province's watersheds.

Internal Assault

While the past has seen some progress in environmental protection, this is the decade of downsizing, decentralization, deregulation, privatization, and deficit-fighting cuts. Every facet of the environment has been negatively affected, as federal and provincial governments bow out, leaving the resource industries to police themselves. Canada's government agencies have been stripped of many of their responsibilities.

Environment Canada, already weak, has recently lost 1,400 employees. It has been rendered impotent by cutbacks in the enforcement of the Canadian Environmental Protection Act, has backtracked on promised legislation to protect endangered species, and has killed its annual report, *The State of Canada's Environment.* Canada has abandoned its earlier promises to stabilize and reduce greenhouse gas emissions. The Ottawa *Citizen* says that Environment Canada "has little influence on anything you eat, drink or breathe."

The federal Department of Natural Resources has "downsized" another 1,500 employees and suffered budget cuts of 69 percent since 1995. Oil and gas exports have been exempted from federal environmental assessments. The Canadian Forest Service is gutting its forestry research centres and reforestation programs.

At Parks Canada, two thousand employees have been laid off and one-third of the budget has been slashed. The Department of Heritage has all but abandoned its program to clean up the hundreds of contaminated sites located in the national parks system. The equivalent of half of one staffperson's time is given annually to this project.

At the Department of Fisheries and Oceans, cuts of 70 percent are starving its world-famous Freshwater Institute. Wetlands and marine biodiversity preservation have been forsaken. One hundred and forty-two distinct races of salmon in Canada's waters have become extinct, while 624 more are at risk.

For five years, the Sierra Club has closely followed Canada's Rio commitments and has given the government of Jean Chrétien an "F" for failing to implement even the most basic of promises. Says the Sierra Club report, "From the beginning, the process was wounded by compromise . . . Five years after the Earth Summit, it is clear that the so-called 'Rio Bargain' has been wholly abrogated by Canada." Executive director Elizabeth May said that the post-Rio meeting was like a family reunion on the *Titanic.*

The provinces are close behind. Environment budgets in Alberta have been slashed by one-third, in Quebec by 50 percent, and in Ontario by 60 percent in the last two years. Most provinces are "reevaluating" every regulation on their books, and massively handing responsibility over to the private sector. Provincial ministries are now allowing industry to self-monitor and propose "solutions" to environmental conflicts. Government's role is being reduced to handing out industry permits setting out allowable levels of direct discharge of pollutants into the air and water.

A July 1997 report by the Commission for Environmental Cooperation, set up by the governments of Mexico, Canada, and the U.S. in the wake of NAFTA, showed that, proportionately, Canadian industrial companies polluted far more than their U.S. counterparts. As well, it named Ontario as the third largest polluter on the continent, worse even than the notorious border areas of Mexico.

Meanwhile, the federal government is steadily devolving to the provinces much of its remaining powers to protect the environment, in the name of "harmonization" to remove regulatory overlap. To facilitate this harmonization, a new level of government, taking the form of the Canadian Council of Ministers of the Environment, has been created. Much to the consternation of environmentalists, this council meets in private, is accountable to no one, and counts many members from the powerful provinces like Ontario that are cutting their environment ministries and regulatory frameworks to the bone.

In proposing a massive program of devolution of power over environmental issues, the council's documents are full of the language of "fiscal realities" and "regional flexibility." Should the program be implemented, the federal government's remaining duties would be limited to providing scientific and technical support, representing Canada's position internationally, and implementing national standards on a limited number of products and substances. Mark Winfield of the Canadian Institute for Environmental Law and Policy says that transferring federal powers to the provinces would require consensus among all the parties; this, he says, would set standards at the lowest common denominator. "It is clear that the agreement [on distribution of powers] would constrain severely the role of the federal government in the protection of Canada's environment. The agreement proposes, for example, the delegation of responsibility for most inspection, and by implication, enforcement, activities related to federal environmental laws to the provinces and territories. This is despite the weak environmental law enforcement records of many of these jurisdictions."

External Assault

The exponential growth of transnational corporations in the natural resource sector, combined with liberalized trade and investment regimes operating to serve their interests, has resulted in an all-out assault on the rights of nation-states, including Canada, and their citizens to protect the natural environment. For these corporations, the MAI is the ultimate weapon in their quest for total freedom.

Transnational corporations control more than 80 percent of the world's land cultivated for export-oriented crops; three to six giant companies control 80 to 90 percent of the world's trade in forest products, iron ore, copper, and precious metals. A handful of petroleum production and refining corporations, the majority American, dominate that sector. These companies, not nation-states or international law, set the conditions for resource extraction and production; by extension, they set environmental standards.

The essence of free trade is deregulation; it becomes next to impossible for a country to place safeguards or conditions on exportable products, including — or perhaps especially — raw materials. Under liberalized investment, the market is given pre-emptive rights to determine the course of resource development, and often no distinction can be made between domestic and foreign investors. Trade regimes like NAFTA, the GATT, and the WTO already have enormous clout in determining environmental, agricultural, land-use, health, and food safety rules, and they are developing tools of trade retaliation that threaten nation-state regulations.

The activities of international trade organizations include attempts to set limits on environmental regulations around the world, with the ultimate goals being to ensure that existing rules are not trade- and profit-inhibiting, and to secure continued access to the world's resources by transnational corporations. Global trade organizations have already successfully used their powers to challenge many national laws. But they also inhibit the consideration of future laws; in anticipation of a trade challenge, a country's bureaucrats and senior politicians will nix proposed national policy before it has even come to public attention.

Further, under international trade rules, there is absolutely no minimum standard of environmental regulation; these rules set ceilings, but not floors. So while countries run the risk of having tough environmental laws disputed under trade agreements, they cannot be challenged for taking no steps to protect the environment, consumer health, or to conserve natural resources. Therefore, domestic standards that are lower than the global average are safer; those that are higher are clear targets.

The effect is that under trade and investment agreements, environmental standards can move in only one direction — downward.

In global trade, no positive weight is given to positive environmental practices. When companies pollute, in effect they appropriate something that belongs to the communities — our clean air and water. Thus the failure of governments to pass environmental standards can be seen as a subsidy to producers who can in this way externalize environmental costs. Because trade agreements establish no minimum standards for environmental regulation, countries are actually encouraged, in some cases, to compete for investment by offering to "subsidize" production by forgoing or even abandoning environmental controls.

The huge benefit to businesses of allowing free access to clean air and water is merely taken for granted. In a highly competitive global trade system in which high standards provide no competitive advantage, many countries are unilaterally dismantling their environmental regulatory structures. (Japan, for instance, recently moved to assimilate the Japanese Environmental Agency into a more powerful ministry. Japanese environmentalists say this will effectively dissolve the agency.)

NAFTA, the GATT, and the WTO have set up a system to knock down not just direct barriers to free trade and investment, but also indirect, or "non-tariff," barriers. These include many of the regulations and laws that have been built up over the years to protect the environment, place controls on foreign ownership of land, and set standards for industrial development.

Together, these trade bodies have weakened Canada's ability to protect its environment and national resources. Three key provisions — most favoured nation, national treatment, and the elimination of restrictions on the volume of traded product —

stipulate that countries must treat "like" products from one country as favourably as those from another, that no distinction can be made between foreign and domestic "like" products, and that quotas or bans imposed for environmental purposes could be challenged as forms of protectionism. Hence, objections to the method of production (called *production and process methods* or PPMs in trade jargon) cannot be used to ban it. This suddenly legalizes a whole host of terrible and inhumane environmental practices, such as the use of drift nets or the clear-cutting of old-growth forests.

As well, environmentalists are concerned that in the case of a conflict, the WTO would take precedence over Multilateral Environmental Agreements (MEAs), like those Canada has signed to ban trade in endangered species (CITES), ozone-depleting substances (Montreal Protocol), and hazardous waste (Basel Convention). Unlike NAFTA, which specifically exempts certain MEAs from trade challenge, the WTO does not recognize their authority; the rules of national treatment, most favoured nation, and quantitative restrictions might, environmentalists fear, prohibit the enforcement of these protocols.

Because the GATT always takes precedence over other trade agreements, including NAFTA, the WTO's lack of MEA exemptions is particularly worrisome. When governments are found to be in breach of their WTO trade obligations, they are subject to retaliatory trade sanctions with substantial financial penalties. And a WTO ruling is automatically implemented unless blocked by a consensus of WTO members.

Says trade expert Steve Shrybman of the West Coast Environmental Law Association, "In the simplest of terms the essential goal of WTO rules is to de-regulate international trade. All WTO agreements set out detailed rules intended to constrain the extent to which governments can regulate international trade, or otherwise 'interfere' with the activities of large corporations. Thus WTO agreements provide extensive lists of things that governments can't do."

MAI Assault

The MAI would continue in the same vein as the other recently adopted trade and investment agreements, including NAFTA and the WTO. Many of its provisions directly mirror these other agreements. But the MAI goes much further. It is an even more radical and extreme document. International trade lawyer Barry Appleton says the MAI is the most aggressive investment treaty in the history of the world. A whole host of federal, provincial, and municipal laws and practices are vulnerable under the MAI, practices such as requiring that recycled content be used in production (a Canadian regulation that paper products have some local recycled content has already been challenged under the GATT), giving preference to environmentally responsible firms in bids for public contracts, limiting mineral extraction and use of unappropriated water to provincial or national residents, and placing restrictions on foreign ownership of land (restrictions of the type that now exist in Prince Edward Island).

Under the MAI, foreign companies operating in Canada would be free to take 100 percent of the after-tax profits they have made from our natural resources out of the country and back to their head offices.

Even the weak rhetorical commitments to the environment that can be found in existing trade agreements would be entirely missing from the MAI. NAFTA's Commission for Environmental Cooperation, though inadequate and without enforcement powers, is emerging as a kind of continental conscience by monitoring the environmental state of the NAFTA countries. The GATT's exemptions for the health of humans, animals, and plant life, and for exhaustible natural resources, though they have been interpreted so narrowly that environmentalists consider them largely worthless, still represent the possibility of introducing environmental concerns into the WTO. In contrast, the MAI contains no general exceptions to protect the environment.

University of Guelph professor John McMurtry explains that the MAI would grant transnational corporations the right "to own any saleable natural resource of other countries and to have national right to any concessions, licence, or authorization to extract its oil, forest, mineral, or other resources with no obligation to sustain these resources, or to use them in the interest of the host society."

Further, these corporations would have the right "to repel as illegal any national standards of human rights, labour rights, or environmental protection on goods produced in and imported from other regions or nations." Several clauses of the MAI (including secondary boycotts and most favoured nation) might prohibit the Canadian government from using investment sanctions against the environmentally harmful practices of another MAI country.

The MAI could thus weaken the growing international practice of using boycotts and withholding pension investments and government procurement contracts to deter companies from investing in countries like Nigeria, whose political leadership has permitted Shell Oil to pollute the homelands of the Ogoni people.

The MAI could allow foreign resource companies to sue governments for enacting or maintaining their own perfectly legal environmental or resource-protection laws. It could even allow them to sue governments who refuse to let them into the country because of a poor environmental record elsewhere. (A U.S. waste treatment corporation, Metalclad, has filed a dispute against Mexico — under the investment provisions of NAFTA — for its refusal to allow the company to operate a notoriously polluting Mexican facility it had bought. The NAFTA provision Metalclad is using has an almost identical counterpart in the MAI.)

Under the MAI, new federal or provincial laws to protect the environment, wilderness, species, or natural resource production could be considered a form of expropriation if they were to have a secondary effect of harming an industry; in such a case, a foreign company operating in Canada could sue for severe damages. Appleton explains, "Rather than have the polluter-pays principle, you now have 'pay the polluter.'"

As environmental writer and researcher Barbara Robson explains, this "effects test" would apply even if the intent of the law were not to discriminate and no identifiable gains were made by other parties. Thus, environmental laws that have sound objectives but are inadvertently harmful to the corporation in question could be challenged under the MAI. An example might be the cancellation of a megaproject involving offshore investment because the project has been demonstrated to have harmful environmental effects.

Perhaps the greatest environmental threat posed by the MAI is in the preferential treatment it would give to foreign investors, whose "expropriation" right to sue for lost profits in the event of new environmental legislation would not be available to domestic firms competing against them. It would soon become advantageous for resource sector transnational corporations to organize themselves in such a way that they are considered "foreign investors" in every country in which they operate. The more a sector like forestry or energy is held by foreign investors, the greater power the private sector would have to stop national governments from enacting legislation considered inimical to its interests.

Energy

A safe, cheap, and dependable supply of energy is crucial to a globalized economy and to the transportation of its goods. The energy sector is tightly controlled by a small handful of global transnationals whose profits are subsidized by taxpayers around the world when governments lease them huge tracts of land and then supply them with funds for exploration. (Just four oil companies have been leased a full two-thirds of Somalia's territory.) Everywhere, the environment is being sacrificed to the benefit of these corporations.

Canada supplies much of North America's energy and, in the FTA and NAFTA, gave away much of its right to control the conditions of its energy exports by removing restrictions on foreign takeovers of Canadian energy companies worth less than $150 million. It was at this time that the industry was deregulated. Astonishingly, the Canadian government agreed to proportional sharing of our energy supplies with the U.S. in perpetuity, or until supplies are gone. The Canadian government cannot reduce the amount of gas and oil exported to Americans without a corresponding reduction to Canadians, even if Canada is experiencing shortages or wishes to meet the requirements of its international climate control treaties. This general proportional sharing clause includes water, which is to be shared with the U.S. in the same manner if Canadian waters are diverted south for American use.

Further, NAFTA prohibits the imposition of energy export taxes that are higher than those for domestic consumers, and exempts government subsidies for oil and gas exploration from trade challenge. These provisions mean that Canadian public funds are used to pay for uncontrolled and environmentally destructive fossil fuel exploration, a process that has already destroyed the habitats of grizzlies, elk, caribou, and many other species, all to the benefit of transnational corporations.

The MAI could remove any power the Canadian government retained in NAFTA to set conditions on foreign investment in the energy sector: it would lift the $150 million ceiling on takeovers, remove the right to impose performance requirements such as employment and domestic content quotas on foreign companies operating in the energy sector, and, because natural resources are included in the MAI definition of an investment, render ineffective the NAFTA reservation to maintain oil and gas situated on federal lands for Canadian-owned companies.

The issue of preferential treatment for foreign investment under the MAI raises serious questions for oil and gas as foreign control in this sector is still very high (45.1 percent in 1995). A powerful foreign-dominated industry could mount an MAI threat that would render financially untenable any attempt by governments in Canada to impose environmental safeguards on the industry, whether by diverting pipeline construction around wildlife habitat, or requiring the construction of double-hold tankers, or taking increased security measures to prevent spills.

As well, governments could not give preferential treatment to the publicly owned energy and hydro-electric enterprises that deliver electricity in most provinces; these utilities in turn would not be allowed to give preferential rates to the citizens of their provinces.

The MAI principles of national treatment and most favoured nation would explicitly apply to the privatization of government energy and hydro-electric facilities. The 25 percent limit on foreign ownership that was placed on Petro-Canada when it was privatized under Mulroney might have to be lifted. Similarly, no share limits could be placed upon the privatization of any provincial hydro-electric facility, and there could be no discrimination against foreign investors in the sale. Ontario premier Mike Harris has promised to privatize Ontario Hydro. Under the MAI, his government could not prevent a foreign corporation from buying it and effectively acquiring control of Niagara Falls, unless that resource is specifically exempted.

The same rules would apply to municipal water and sewer systems, now financed by local taxpayers. Shrinking provincial transfer payments have caused municipalities across the country to consider privatizing these services; *The Globe and Mail* reports that Canada has become "a hot prospect for foreign water firms." Under the MAI, there might be no way to control this process or keep these vital services in Canadian hands. Canada is one of a handful of countries to allow provinces and municipalities to cede control of energy services without policy constraints from higher levels of government. Once they are gone, they will not be retrievable.

Climate Change

The Chrétien government admits that it has failed to live up to its 1992 Rio commitment to stabilize greenhouse gas emissions at 1990 levels by the year 2000, its Red Book promise to reduce carbon dioxide emissions by 20 percent by 2005, or its 1993 election promise to give the renewable-energy sector tax advantages equal to those now accorded the fossil fuel industry. This failure to meet such modest targets is deeply troubling, given the need for far more decisive action. Global warming has been identified by scientists as a potential ecological disaster. But the WTO and the MAI promise to be major impediments to the collective action the world urgently needs if this disaster is to be avoided. Several cases illustrate how.

The very first ruling of the WTO was in a 1996 case against a U.S. clean air environmental law on gasoline contaminants. This law, mandated by the Environmental Protection Agency (EPA), required the cleanliness of gasoline sold in U.S. cities to improve by 15 percent over 1990 levels and set a timetable for rural America as well. It was passed to cut down on emissions that produce smog and toxic air pollutants.

The EPA imposed slightly tougher import restrictions on foreign producers of lower-grade gasoline than on American companies, which had spent billions of dollars in their refineries in anticipation of the law, and were already producing gasoline of a relatively higher standard. Venezuela and Brazil challenged this differential treatment at the WTO, claiming the U.S. law violated the WTO's national treatment provision, and won. The ruling left the U.S. with a choice between accepting lower-standard foreign gasoline or facing $150 million in annual trade sanctions.

A similar challenge under the investment provisions of NAFTA has been launched against Canada by the U.S. manufacturer of another gasoline additive and is a specific example of the kind of threat that will be possible under the MAI. In 1997, Canada banned the importation and transport of MMT, a manganese fuel additive considered a dangerous neurotoxin that also interferes with the diagnostic system in cars that controls anti-pollution devices. Thus MMT at once increases air pollution and potentially delivers a poison to the human brain. The American maker of MMT (as well as leaded gasoline), Ethyl Corporation, has sued the Canadian government under NAFTA's Chapter 11 investor-state provisions, which allow any corporation of the NAFTA countries to sue any of the governments for failing to uphold their "rights" as enshrined in the agreement. Ethyl is asking for nearly $350 million in damages, arguing that the ban constitutes an illegitimate expropriation of its assets.

If Ethyl wins, Canadian taxpayers will have to foot the bill arising from the contestation of a piece of legislation intended to protect our health and the environment, legislation that the government should have every right to enact. U.S.-based Friends of the Earth asks if this is not a case of "ban a poison, pay the poisoners" and points out that it serves as a precedent for the MAI:

> Every time a country bans a potentially toxic substance, a foreign company that was a major manufacturer of the substance could expect to be compensated . . .
>
> A precedent will be set whereby the legal right of corporations to be compensated when public health regulations affect a company's bottom line is given the same weight as the public's right not to be harmed by industrial toxins. This could send the message to investors that seeking compensation from the public for the cost of complying with environmental regulations constitutes a legitimate business strategy.

Ethyl submitted an intent to file six months before the MMT ban was passed in Canada, signifying that its plan was to influence the government not to pass the law.

The MAI would encourage this practice and would also permit companies to sue not just for actual losses but also for future losses; further, they could claim, as Ethyl is doing, that the case itself has hurt their international reputation, and seek damages for that.

Forests

Exports in the Canadian forest sector have exploded, increasing by 57 percent between 1993 and 1996 alone. At the same time, Canada has switched almost entirely to clear-cutting; 90 percent of forest products in this country are harvested through clear-cutting — that's twice the proportion in 1950. Ninety-three percent of all U.S. imports of wood pulp come from Canadian clear-cutting, and 90 percent of the area logged each year in Canada is virgin forest.

Elizabeth May, in her disturbing and passionate new book, *At the Cutting Edge,* the story of Canada's abuse of its forest heritage, says our forests are in crisis. We are witnessing corporate short-term rape of the resource, says May, open to the highest bidder. One-fifth of Manitoba is under corporate lease; Alberta has signed corporate leases to develop land the size of Great Britain; Ontario is logging its last old-growth forest. The story is the same across the country.

It is less known that as this is happening, the sector is increasingly dominated by foreign-based transnational corporations. The rise in foreign control in this industry is dramatic: in 1988, 70 percent of the capital employed in the wood and paper sector was Canadian, and 30 percent was foreign-owned; by 1993, the most recent year for which there are statistics, foreign ownership had grown to 46 percent. If this trend has continued, and recent mergers and takeovers suggest it has, *the proportion of the forestry sector under foreign control is now probably well over 50 percent.*

Many environmentalists have stopped asking the origin of a corporation; they understandably say that Canadians produce our very own world-class polluters, and it matters little to the earth whether a company dumping toxic waste or clear-cutting virgin forest is "theirs" or "ours." However, it very much matters who owns the resource when the WTO and the MAI give preferential treatment to foreign investors. Domestic companies are obliged to follow a country's domestic laws. Foreign companies, although they are also subject to the domestic laws of their host countries, would, through the MAI, be given powerful new weapons with which to attack these domestic laws.

Several previous trade disputes have established the right of foreign investors to our resources. Even though NAFTA explicitly exempts log export controls from the rules of free trade, the U.S. has already challenged a Canadian ban on raw log exports as an unfair subsidy, claiming that the Canadian companies could make value-added profits on their processed logs. The panel sided with the U.S. More recently, a GATT dispute panel forced Indonesia to lift its ban on the export of raw logs. Shrybman says that the effects of these rulings will be felt in all the resource sectors, where governments will have to assure foreign industries the same access to their resources as is made available to their own citizens.

But the MAI could go a dangerous step further. Elizabeth May poses a scenario in which Canadians finally understand the looming crisis of wood shortage in Canada and realize that most of these companies are operating on publicly held common land. Canadians demand an end to clear-cutting, or the raising of stumpage fees (the system by which logging companies lease their rights from the Crown), or the imposition of strict rules on logging practices to protect rivers and fish. *But if provincial or federal governments try to enact such laws under the MAI, foreign forestry companies could consider the laws a form of expropriation and sue for lost profits.* New Zealand's Fletcher Challenge, Japan's Daishawa, and America's Weyerhauser and Abitibi Consolidated could arguably have more say over Canadian forests than any government in the country.

Fisheries

The same situation could arise under the MAI if Canada tried to apply the Federal Fisheries Act to the behaviour of a foreign-based company. This act is arguably the strongest piece of environmental legislation in Canada, making it illegal to put into fish-bearing water any substance that is deleterious to the health of the fish. Technically, under the MAI, any foreign company operating in Canada would have to abide by this law as it was in force before the MAI. However, this act has been unevenly enforced. The St. Lawrence River is an open sewer; the City of Montreal dumps its raw sewage into the St. Lawrence and the chemical companies that line its banks dump their toxins. As another example, if B.C. were to enforce this act, many of its current logging practices would be deemed illegal.

Under the MAI, however, foreign companies forbidden to dump wastes and chemicals could refuse to comply with the act if some Canadian companies were still allowed to pollute; they could claim that they were being discriminated against because Canadian companies had not been consistently forced to comply. This, in turn, could render the Federal Fisheries Act difficult to enforce at all.

Further, the MAI contains no protections from the principle

of national treatment when it comes to access to natural resources. Canada's right to use export controls to manage its fisheries has already been struck down in two important cases, one through the FTA and the other through the GATT. The cases concerned the eighty-year-old practice requiring salmon and herring caught in Canadian waters to be landed in Canada for inspection, biological sampling, and processing. (This practice was considered necessary for the conservation of the species as well as to provide employment for Canadian workers.)

The decisions of the panels allowed U.S. packing ships (floating fish-processing factories) to operate freely in Canadian waters and with precisely the same claim to Canadian fish as Canadian packers enjoy. However, the decision didn't affect Canada's right to reserve commercial fishing licences and access to Canadian fisheries for Canadians, a practice allowed under NAFTA and widely used by all provinces to protect Canadian sovereignty over its fisheries. Under the MAI, however, Canada might not be able to restrict foreign fishing fleets from operating fully in our waters.

Species and Wilderness

The fight to save the world's endangered species and wilderness spaces is at risk under the MAI. International state-sanctioned bans to protect endangered species might not be permitted by the MAI if the bans interfered with the trade or investment interests of a member country or corporation. As a result, an important tool in species protection would be lost; countries that are concerned about Canada's treatment of its embattled wildlife would no longer be able to threaten the Canadian government with trade retaliation for failing to adopt protective legislation.

The MAI, like the WTO, might take precedence over environmental treaties like the Convention on International Trade in Endangered Species of Wild Fauna and Flora (CITES). Because "like" products must be treated as equals, no matter the conditions of production, countries could no longer ban a product because it was harvested cruelly, or harmed endangered species or the environment.

The GATT has already struck down the U.S. Marine Mammal Protection Act because it banned the import of tuna caught in Mexican and European drift nets that also kill dolphins. Canada, to its shame, supported the GATT challenge. In 1993, the U.S. warned of a trade dispute over Canada's ban on the import of dogs from American "puppy mills" that had much lower standards than Canadian mills; Canada backed down and weakened its own standards.

Norway has threatened WTO action if other countries impose trade sanctions against it for violating the global ban on commercial whaling. Four Asian nations are challenging the recent U.S. ban on the import of their shrimp, which are caught with methods that slaughter endangered sea turtles.

Not only are endangered-species protection laws of many countries at risk; so too, are regulations over the humane treatment and slaughter of farm animals. Under the MAI's "like" treatment provisions, a foreign investor in Canada whose standards of animal treatment did not meet Canadian standards could use the treaty to challenge Canada's laws.

In another, very important example, Canada has (so far) refused to grant the giant chemical company, Monsanto, the right to market bovine growth hormone (BGH), a drug to increase milk production in cows, in Canada. There is strong evidence that the injection of BGH into dairy cows is a serious threat to animal health, and links have been established between a by-product of BGH, IGF-1, and breast and colon cancer in humans. The Europeans have banned BGH until tests prove that it is not harmful to human or animal health. But Canada's NAFTA partners, the U.S. and Mexico, have allowed the production and sale of BGH, and Monsanto says that, under NAFTA, Canada's refusal is not based on legitimate scientific proof, but is being used as a form of protectionism for the Canadian dairy industry.

Two recent trade disputes will have a direct impact on this case. Canada and the U.S. launched and won, in 1997, a challenge before the WTO to a similar European ban on North American beef treated with another (flesh-related) type of hormone. The EU must now allow imports of this beef or pay compensation to the North American beef industry. A similar challenge against Canada's ban on BGH might result in a similar decision.

In September 1997, just months after that WTO ruling, the U.S. dairy industry announced it was launching a WTO challenge to the import quota on fluid milk that Canada has used for decades to protect the industry. If the U.S. wins the case, American milk imports will pour across the Canadian border. If, at that time, the MAI is in place, Canada might have no right and no way to prevent BGH-enhanced milk and milk products from coming into the country. Forcing U.S. imports to meet certain standards could be considered an illegal government "taking," if arbitrators consider our "science" inadequate.

As well, under the MAI, if a province or the federal government were to create new wilderness conservation areas or public parks, they might have to pay foreign investors with interest in the sites potentially prohibitive expropriation reparations. Under the MAI, the acquisition of land for preservation and conservation would not be a protected activity, whereas the purchase of virgin forest by a logging corporation for commercial purposes is.

A further threat is to Canada's parks system, now underfunded and endangered by commercial interests. The Canadian government has set up a new parks administration that will run on a commercial basis. Ontario has created a new organization, called "Ontario Parks," to manage the province's parks. A partnership between the provincial government and the private sector, it has a "marketing office" that will promote corporate sponsorships of the system. Under the MAI, once Canada's parks are operating as "for-profits," they would not be able to be reserved for Canadian investors. Disney markets our Mounties; there is no reason to suppose it won't one day operate Banff.

Finally, the practice of balancing economic development with sound land resource management is threatened by the MAI. Many provinces limit the sale of public land and resources and also regulate how private landowners may develop their property. Says constitutional and trade law expert Robert Stumberg of the Georgetown University Law Center, land development is an investment that clearly would fall within the jurisdiction of the MAI; foreign landowners could argue that land use restrictions reduce the value of their property, and as such, constitute a form of "taking." Zoning controls to protect wetlands or habitats for endangered species could be challenged as well.

Pesticides and Toxins

Free trade has already reduced pesticide standards in Canada and elsewhere; regulations to control pesticides and toxins are now considered trade irritants, not health and environmental issues, and are subject to a whole host of trade disputes. Pesticide standards are now subject to a special provision of the WTO (the

Agreement on the Application of Sanitary and Phytosanitary Measures) that requires a consensus of international scientific opinion as a necessary precondition for nation-state environmental regulation. But the MAI would give the chemical corporations a powerful weapon to use against government regulation.

The Canadian federal Pest Control Products Act registers chemicals for use as pesticides. The law is badly flawed in that it contains no process to deregister a chemical that has been proven harmful since it was registered. Furthermore, the act's appeal process is open only to the companies seeking registration, not to environmentalists or others who oppose a particular application. Nevertheless, from time to time, Canada has banned a chemical after overwhelming evidence of its harm. This was the case in the mid-1980s when the environment minister under Mulroney decided to ban the pesticide Alachlor, made by Monsanto, the same U.S. company that manufactured Agent Orange and now makes BGH. Monsanto appealed the ruling but the minister confirmed the decision to keep Alachlor out of Canada. Under the MAI, however, Monsanto could argue that this law is a form of expropriation and demand onerous compensation. The same story would apply to toxic substances that Canada regulates under the Canadian Environmental Protection Act.

Mining

Finally, a word about a similar story in the mining sector. As in forestry and energy, foreign control in mining and metals is steadily increasing. In 1988, 30.53 percent of the sector was foreign-controlled. This rose to 37.38 percent by 1993. In 1996, the largest foreign-based companies increased their budgets for Canada by almost 45 percent compared with the previous year. These foreign-based companies would be given special status under the MAI, allowing them to exert a disproportionate amount of pressure on the federal and provincial governments to deregulate the sector.

Barry Appleton gives a striking example. An American company operates a gold mine in Canada; it is leaching contaminants. The government moves to ban this practice, or shuts the company down under existing law. *Under the MAI (and, to an extent, NAFTA and the WTO) the government would have to compensate the company fully and immediately.* In such a scenario, Ottawa could end up paying more in compensation than it takes in penalties, and the company could claim damages for the full worth of the gold mine if it has to shut down as a result of the government action. None of these recourses is available to domestic companies.

This scenario could unfold in cash-strapped developing countries, where our own mining companies — like Placer Dome, which has been involved in environmental controversy in the Philippines, and Peter Munk's Barrick Gold — have an inordinate amount of wealth and influence. These companies, often subsidized by the Canadian Export Development Corporation, are operating in more than one hundred countries, some so desperate for foreign investment that they have done away with environmental laws and leased huge tracts of land in perpetuity to these Canadian investors.

The government of the Philippines has passed a law that perfectly anticipates the kind of rights these mining companies and other resource transnationals would have in an MAI world. Roughly 40 percent of the country's entire land area has been set aside for lease to foreign mining corporations like Placer Dome. They would have exclusive rights to explore and mine this land for twenty-five years, renewable for a further twenty-five, and they would be granted 100 percent control of equity. They would receive a five-year tax holiday, renewable every five years, 100 percent repatriation of profits, attendant water and timber rights, easement rights to evict communities, and the right to settle their own labour disputes without government interference.

This, then, is the heart of the environmental argument against the MAI. It is not a case of "wonderful Canada," with its excellent environmental record, vs. "terrible U.S.," with its inferior record and bad transnationals. In some cases, Canadian laws are superior; in other cases, U.S. laws are to be preferred. The real story of the MAI is that it could be used, even more than NAFTA and the WTO are already being used, to knock down environmental standards wherever they are found.

In fact, Canada's motives for promoting the MAI are no different from the motives of the U.S. or the other OECD countries. All seek to extend the reach of their transnationals in a competitive world. All want to be "players" in a system few bother to question. And all seem to be willing to sacrifice their responsibility to the environment to get there.

The loss is the earth's.

FIVE

THE DEMISE OF
SOCIAL RIGHTS

*"Social security has become accepted as one of the things for
which the people of the world are fighting. It is one of the
concrete expressions of a better world."*
— LEONARD MARSH IN THE 1943
REPORT ON SOCIAL SECURITY FOR CANADA

In Canada, citizens have been
fortunate to have many of their basic social needs met by their
democratically elected governments and the institutions they
have put in place. But the people's right to these social institutions did not come without generations of struggle. The driving
force behind this struggle was what the Universal Declaration of
Human Rights called the dignity of the human person. All
citizens, by virtue of their status as human beings, have basic
social rights such as access to adequate food, clothing, and
shelter, along with employment, education, and health care and
other public services like consumer and environmental protection. Indeed, the realization of these and related social rights has

long been considered essential for citizens to participate in the building up of their communities and democratic societies in general.

Naturally, the state had a pivotal role to play in the establishment of these basic social rights. In Canada, this called for the development of a public sector that would redistribute the nation's wealth among citizens and regions and provide universal access to services that would enhance people's social rights. Between the 1930s and the 1970s, the federal and provincial governments created a body of social legislation, as well as a variety of public institutions and enterprises to deliver social services. Although these initiatives have certainly been laced with imperfections, they did establish social rights as a cornerstone of democracy.

Social Legacy

The blueprint for social rights in Canada was put forward during World War II by the Marsh Report on Social Security in Canada, which called for the pooling of federal government benefits for maternity, sickness, unemployment, and old age pensions into one, universal, comprehensive social insurance plan for all Canadians. The foundation of a comprehensive social security plan, declared the Marsh Report, is a policy of full employment buttressed by a comprehensive health insurance program for all Canadians, fully funded federal assistance programs for the unemployed, and a universal system of children's allowances. At the same time, the Marsh Report was strengthened by two other major commissions, namely, the Heagerty Report on Health Insurance, which proposed that all Canadians be eligible for medical, dental, pharmaceutical, hospital, and nursing services, and the Curtis Report on Housing and Community Planning, which called for public intervention by governments to provide low-income housing.

The first universal social program to show that Ottawa was beginning to assume a measure of responsibility for Canadian families was Family Allowance. Launched in 1945, Family Allowance then provided 20 percent of the average income for a family of three. It was followed by the Old Age Security program in 1952 and a limited form of public health insurance in 1957. The Unemployment Assistance Act marked the first legislated program for relief initiated by both the federal and provincial governments. But it was not until the 1960s that a comprehensive system was put in place to ensure that, at least to a certain extent, the social rights of Canadians were met. The Canada Assistance Plan gave Ottawa a mandate to alleviate poverty in the country and provided all Canadians in need with the right to claim social assistance. The Canada Pension Plan enhanced the social rights of seniors by adding a wage-related supplement to their Old Age Security, increasing benefits in line with increases in the cost of living, and including those who were widowed or had long-term disabilities. The Medical Care Act of 1966 established a non-profit, comprehensive, and universally available health care system for all Canadians, thereby becoming arguably the most significant universal social program in the country. In addition, legislative action was taken by both Ottawa and the provinces to improve public education, provide social housing, and ensure consumer protection.

By the 1990s, however, the social rights of Canadians were under full-scale attack. Eliminating government deficits had become the number one priority in Ottawa and the provincial capitals. And the Business Council on National Issues had been successful in its bid to make social spending the main target in Canada's battle against government deficits. Studies by Statistics Canada had shown the prime causes of government deficits to be rising unemployment, high interest rates, and lower corporate taxes. Nevertheless, massive cuts in government spending on social programs and public services became the order of the day. The single biggest blow came in the 1995 federal budget when finance minister Paul Martin introduced the Canada Health and Social Transfer Act (CHST), which, in effect, chopped a whopping 40 percent out of federal cash transfer payments to the provinces for health care, social assistance, and post-secondary education over a three-year period. What's more, a recent study by Statistics Canada shows that social transfer cuts disproportionately affect women. Between 1992 and 1995, the percentage of women who relied on social transfers rather than employment income rose sharply from 48 to 67 percent.

During the same period, the new free trade regime was placing pressure on Canadian governments to harmonize the country's social programs with (lower) U.S. standards. Take, for example, unemployment insurance. Before the FTA, Canada had a much more comprehensive and generous UI program than did the U.S. Indeed, 87 percent of unemployed Canadians were eligible for UI benefits compared with only 52 percent in the U.S. A consortium of U.S. corporations threatened to challenge Canada's UI program as an "unfair trade subsidy" because, unlike in the American program, the federal government was a major funding partner, thereby giving Canadian businesses and workers an economic advantage. At the same time, big business coalitions like the BCNI were demanding that Ottawa take action to substantially reduce its UI benefits and limit eligibility. Immediately after the FTA was ratified in 1989, the Mulroney government tabled legislation to roll back Canada's UI program, including the withdrawal of Ottawa as one of the three principal funding partners. By 1996, after three more sets of UI reforms, less than 40 percent of unemployed Canadians were eligible, and for what had become much lower benefits.

External Threats

Subsequent free trade institutions like NAFTA and the WTO, which also cover cross-border trade in services, threaten to reinforce this disintegration of social rights. Although Ottawa has attempted to exempt Canada's health and social services from these trade regimes, the protection provided is very limited. In NAFTA, the much touted exemption that Ottawa negotiated to protect health care, education, and other social services (Annex II-C-9) is general and full of loopholes. It does not apply, for example, to the NAFTA rules for financial services, which cover the insurance industry, or to the NAFTA sections on intellectual property rights, which secure patent protections for drug and chemical manufacturers. And because this exemption does not apply to NAFTA's rules for public enterprises, it is even more difficult for Ottawa or the provinces to establish new universal social programs like public automobile insurance.

Ottawa is likely to request that Canada's health and social services be exempted from the MAI rules, but economist Andrew Jackson maintains that such a NAFTA-like exemption would be completely inadequate, as it fails to take into account the complexity of our systems for the delivery of public and social services. In Washington, the U.S. trade representative has made it crystal clear that the NAFTA general exemption "covers only services delivered directly by governments, and not services characterized as a mixture of public, private, and not-for-profit delivery." Canada's system of health and social services, argues Jackson, is just that — a complex mix of public, private, and not-for-profit delivery. Jackson cites a legal opinion prepared by Dr. Bryan Schwartz of the University of Manitoba, who concluded that the NAFTA exemption pertaining to a "social service delivered for a public purpose" would not be sufficient to protect health and social services in Canada where there have been massive government cutbacks along with deregulation and partial privatization.

Jackson also says that the MAI would go beyond NAFTA in terms of its implications for social and public services by both broadening the definition of investment and extending the principle of national treatment to subsidies. The MAI thus poses "a clear threat to the maintenance of not-for-profit public and social services. The MAI could give foreign investors the right to establish for-profit enterprises in the social and health service area — particularly in areas of mixed public/private delivery. Further, the MAI could allow foreign investors to challenge government support of not-for-profit providers of social and public services" as a direct violation of the national treatment principle. Since a considerable portion of Canada's health (e.g., hospitals and community health clinics), social (e.g., elder care, child care, and home care), and education services are delivered by not-for-profit agencies, this sector could become a major target under the MAI.

Meanwhile, a growing number of for-profit transnational corporations are moving into the fields of health, education, and social services. In countries like Canada, the privatization of these now publicly funded services would open up a multi-billion-dollar market for such corporations. In short, these corporations are emerging as the Trojan horse inside the public sector. The MAI would simply accelerate corporate takeover of social programs and public services. Although an investment treaty like this is technically not supposed to have any direct bearing on the social programs of nation-states, the MAI proposals certainly provide tools for corporations to dismantle the various social rights now enjoyed by Canadian citizens.

Health Care

Canadians have good reason to fear the future of our cherished public health care system. The five principles of the Canada Health Act — accessibility, universality, comprehensiveness, public funding, and public administration — are not fully protected under any of the new trade regimes. The proposed MAI rules would open up new opportunities for private, profit-oriented health care corporations to move in and take over pieces of Canada's medicare system. After all, viewed from the perspective of the private health care industry, Canada has a lucrative $72 billion market, 72 percent of which is funded each year by governments through public revenues. (More recent figures show that government funding has now slipped to 68 percent.)

Under the CHST, the massive cuts in federal transfer payments for provincial health care plans have already set the stage for the privatization of medical services. The cuts have forced provincial governments to close down hospitals and de-list health services and pharmaceutical drugs previously covered by medicare. When medical services and drugs are de-listed from the public health care system, the market is open for private insurance companies like Liberty Health and Metropolitan Life. And when hospitals are shut down, companies like Columbia/HCA, the largest for-profit hospital chain in the U.S., can move in to set up private hospital services not on the basis of people's need but on their ability to pay.

Investment consulting firms like Lehman Brothers actually documented the strategies used by private insurance, hospital, pharmaceutical, and medical product companies in taking control of the health care market in the U.S. during the 1970s and 1980s. Reports Lehman Brothers, for-profit health care corporations soon became "the gatekeepers of the health care dollar, . . . dictat[ing] the direction of health care spending" in the U.S. It now appears that similar investment strategies are being deployed here in Canada. As health care analyst Colleen Fuller reports, a Canadian-owned corporation known as MDS has suddenly emerged as a major player in the private health care industry, providing services to 17,000 physicians and institutions through 380 locations in seven provinces. In 1996, MDS announced joint ventures with hospital chain Columbia/HCA and pharmaceutical giant Bristol-Myers Squibb. Furthermore, the world's largest management consulting firm, KPMG, which masterminded the drive to privatize hospitals in London, England, has been hired to do the same in Canada.

These and related investment strategies for the corporate takeover of Canada's public health care system would be greatly facilitated if the MAI proposals are adopted and ratified. Increasingly, publicly funded health care institutions ranging from hospitals to clinics would be compelled to operate as commercial enterprises. Provincial government procurement of health care services, which involves the expenditure of several billions of public dollars every year, would be subject to MAI restrictions on performance requirements. Community-based health care, for example, would by definition be out-of-bounds as local content would be considered a performance requirement. Similarly, the procedures to be followed in the privatization of public enterprises would give foreign-based hospital chains and insurance corporations the tools they need to capture new health care markets in Canada. There is also nothing to prevent health maintenance organizations (HMOs), which have mushroomed into a major part of the private health care industry in the U.S., from making use of these MAI tools to pry open new markets here in Canada.

Following an aggressive lobbying campaign in 1993, the giants of the pharmaceutical industry (including Eli Lilly, Merck, Pfizer, and Bristol-Myers Squibb) succeeded in winning monopoly protection in Canada for their drug patents, a monopoly that was later cemented in the intellectual property rights sections of NAFTA. The MAI's provisions for intellectual property rights could permit the pharmaceutical industry to reinforce its monopoly protection on drug patents. And under the MAI, the Chrétien government could face serious obstacles if it proceeded with its election promise to expand Canada's public health care system by adding a pharmacare program to provide Canadians with free prescription drugs. To provide this service on a low-cost basis, Ottawa would likely want to strike a deal with Canada's generic drug industry, thereby discriminating against foreign investors. Not only would such a move be seen as a direct violation of MAI rules, but transnational pharmaceutical companies could invoke the standstill clause or charge the government with expropriation without compensation.

To make matters worse, transnational corporations in pharmaceutical, chemical, and other industries would likely take advantage of the MAI's added protection measures for intellectual property rights, to consolidate their control over research, equipment, and product manufacturing in the health care field. Potentially, these protection measures could involve not only compulsory licencing, which is designed to protect the established pharmaceutical and chemical industries and their monopoly control over scientific research, but also the patenting of life forms, which could have profound implications for health care in the future.

Even if our negotiators were able to achieve a NAFTA-like exemption for the Canada Health Act, it would not be comprehensive enough to cover the complexities of a mixed public, private, and not-for-profit system like Canada's. Nor would the exemption be applicable to all the MAI rules. What's more, foreign-based private health care corporations could pressure Ottawa to roll back pieces of the Canada Health Act that are "non-conforming" to MAI rules. It is not yet clear whether provincial governments would be given the opportunity, as they were with NAFTA, to exempt their own health insurance plans and related health care services from the MAI rules.

Meanwhile, Quebec's new family and social policy program, which involves granting subsidies to non-profit community child care facilities, could be charged as a violation of the MAI national treatment rules on subsidies. At the very least, Quebec would have to make these subsidies available to foreign-owned companies providing similar services. The range of government subsidy programs that exist in other provinces for non-profit health care services could be similarly affected. In addition, transnationals could challenge many of the federal health-related programs highlighted in the Chrétien government's Red Book II. These programs involve granting hundreds of millions of dollars in subsidies to non-profit institutions for the delivery of health services, and include the National AIDS Strategy, the Tobacco

Demand Reduction Strategy, the Canadian Breast Cancer Initiative, the Vocational Rehabilitation of Disabled Persons and Canada Prenatal Nutrition programs, plus the major grant promised for non-insured health services for aboriginal peoples.

Public Education

Canadians also place a high premium on universal access to quality public education. But this cherished social right is in jeopardy. In virtually every province, massive government cutbacks to public and post-secondary education have compelled cash-strapped schools, colleges, and universities to throw themselves on the mercy of private corporations. In exchange, corporations are gaining access to a new generation of consumers, young people who spend up to 40 percent of their time each day in school or college. Here again, the MAI would help foreign-based corporations pry open this lucrative market. Indeed, Canada's public education system now represents an estimated $60 billion annual market. In the U.S., corporations are moving into public education, creating a whole new for-profit education industry. Investment firms like Lehman Brothers are providing corporations with a road map of the education market and investment opportunities generated by increased privatization. Meanwhile, across Canada, more than 20,000 school-business partnerships have been formed. No longer able to afford adequate supplies or technical equipment to meet education needs, school boards are entering into "partnerships" with technology and communications corporations like AT&T, IBM, General Electric, Hewlett Packard, and Unitel, as well as Bell Canada and Northern Telecom. Similarly, school boards lacking funds for lunch programs or cafeteria services are forming partnerships with food and beverage companies like Burger King, Coca-Cola, McDonald's, PepsiCo, and Pizza Hut.

Wary of these new partnerships with corporations, many school boards, colleges, and universities have tried to establish guidelines and standards for regulating the practices of sponsoring companies and holding them accountable. But even regulating these school-business partnerships could run afoul of the new investment regime. Suppose, for example, that a school or college board wanted to apply strict limits on the advertising and marketing practices of foreign-based corporations, as well as on their access to curriculum development. As agents of provincial governments, it is conceivable that these school and college boards could be charged with violating MAI rules by imposing performance standards on foreign-based corporations. Moreover, the purchase of educational materials and services by provincial governments and their school or college institutions could not be restricted to domestic companies but would have to be opened up to foreign corporations as well.

The MAI rules might also be used to pressure provincial governments into accepting private educational institutions. Under the agreement, a foreign investor involved in the promotion of charter schools in Canada (schools designed to attract a certain type of student by means of a particular philosophy and teaching method) could demand the same access to public financing from provincial governments as public schools. Similarly, a provincial government sponsoring a worker training program, or an educational program for new immigrants, could not favour a community college over a foreign-owned institute. Nor could a provincial government (let alone a school or college board) adopt a policy of maintaining Canadian content in the development of curriculum or the use of educational materials.

Social Assistance

The demise of social rights has been felt, perhaps most acutely, by Canada's poor. Despite its many flaws, the Canada Assistance Plan (CAP) declared that every citizen in need had a right to social assistance, especially for the basics of life such as food, clothing, and shelter. With this entitlement, the distinction between "deserving" and "undeserving" poor was erased. Under CAP, it did not matter whether one's need for social assistance was based on a disability, or an inability to find work, or ineligibility for unemployment insurance. Not only was CAP designed to consolidate a patchwork of welfare programs into a common program with national standards, but it was based on a cost-sharing formula so that, in times of recession, expanding welfare costs would be borne equally by Ottawa and the provinces. But the Canada Assistance Plan was effectively dismantled by the introduction of the CHST under the Chrétien government.

The CHST not only terminated the cost-sharing formula for social assistance, but saw to it that federal transfer funds would no longer be earmarked for the needs of the poor. Federal transfer payments would be made in the form of a much smaller block grant, allowing the provinces to decide what amounts are allocated to health, education, and social assistance. Under these political circumstances, the lion's share of the shrunken pot would go to health and education, not to social assistance for low-income families, disabled people, poor children, or the working poor. Provincial governments no longer have to meet national standards in delivering social assistance; instead, several are now giving priority to workfare rather than welfare. Yet, workfare really amounts to nothing less than a cash cow for business. Essentially it provides subsidies to employers for hiring people at low wages and creates a pool of cheap labour. It has also proven to be an effective mechanism for keeping wages down and profits up.

In the U.S., big corporations are now cashing in on multi-billion-dollar government welfare and workfare programs. Corporations ranging from the giant defence manufacturer Lockheed Martin to Electrical Data Systems, Andersen Consulting, Unisys, and a host of smaller companies are getting into the welfare business. State governments are beginning to privatize parts of their welfare programs. Lockheed, for example, has taken over the business of collecting child support and fingerprinting welfare recipients in several states. Job brokerage firms like America Works have been busy propelling welfare recipients into workfare programs in cities like Buffalo and San Francisco. Now that the Clinton administration's welfare reform package has been passed by Congress, the big push is on to privatize parts of the system and allow corporations to cash in on the public revenues and profits to be made on the backs of the poor.

However repugnant Canadians may find these U.S. trends, the fact remains that social assistance could also become a profit-making business for corporations in this country. Indeed, the stage has already been set by the dismantling of CAP and the replacement of welfare with workfare. Companies like Andersen Consulting have begun to secure contracts with provincial governments in Canada, notably New Brunswick and Ontario. If U.S. giants like Lockheed decided to invest heavily in the welfare business, the MAI would certainly provide them with the tools they need to break into open markets elsewhere, including Canada. Given the performance requirement restrictions of the MAI, for example, foreign enterprises like Andersen Consulting would likely be eligible for service contracts issued by provincial governments. If a province decided to privatize a major piece of its welfare program, corporations like Lockheed could make use of the MAI rules on the privatization of public enterprises to secure control over this new market. Meanwhile, the MAI's investor-state dispute mechanism could be used to pressure provincial governments to move more aggressively in this direction.

Public Pensions

An adequate level of retirement income for senior citizens has been one of the key goals in the struggle for social rights in Canada. Today, public programs like Old Age Security (OAS), the Guaranteed Income Supplement (GIS), and the Canada Pension Plan (CPP) on average account for at least half of the total income received by Canadians over the age of sixty-five. Through these and related programs, considerable progress has been made in reducing poverty among elderly Canadians. Yet, more than 20 percent of senior citizens still live below the poverty line, 50 percent of whom are single, mostly women. In the future, this elderly poverty rate is bound to grow; between now and the year 2030, Canada's over-sixty-five population is expected to double. But instead of strengthening and expanding Canada's public pension system in light of these predictions, various forces are acting to dismantle and privatize it.

In recent years, the Reform Party has been waging a relentless campaign against the CPP. The Reform plan proposes that individual Canadians develop their own retirement income packages by investing in mutual funds and the stock market. In many ways, these proposals are based on the private pension model devised in Chile under the regime of General Pinochet. Reform's campaign has also been largely backed by key elements of big business, including the C. D. Howe Institute, a prominent policy think tank funded by some of Canada's major corporations, and the Earnscliffe Strategy Group, an influential public relations firm with close ties to the federal Finance Department.

Although the Chrétien government has not officially adopted these proposals, it has begun to move in this direction by calling for the gradual elimination of OAS (in the 1996 federal budget) and the management of the multi-billion-dollar CPP fund by private investment firms (in the 1997 federal budget). Besides Chile, countries like Mexico have begun to turn the management of their public pension funds over to private investment firms as well. An increasing number, including Japan, Singapore, Sweden, Argentina, and Peru, are also investing a substantial portion of their public pension funds in the private stock market. As these trends towards private management and investment continue, it becomes increasingly likely that public pensions would be subject to the MAI rules of investment, all the more so since many of these private investment firms are foreign-owned.

Over the next ten years, it is estimated that the CPP investment fund will balloon from $40 billion today to approximately $120 billion. If this transpires, the CPP would be holding a block of capital worth as much as the seven largest mutual fund companies combined. In the past, the CPP fund has been a source of capital for provincial governments; they could invest the capital in bonds and generate a return for the fund. But once the CPP is being managed by private investment firms, a substantial portion of its funds will be invested on the open stock market. If Ottawa, however, should decide to reserve a major percentage of the CPP fund exclusively for provincial government bonds, foreign investment firms or banks could challenge such requirements as a violation of MAI investment rules dealing with financial services.

At the same time, any government policies calling for a portion of these pension funds to be invested in community development or used to promote social responsibility could be struck down because they impose performance standards on capital for investment. The MAI could also be used against the federal government's 20 percent limit on the amount of RRSP funds that can go towards foreign investments. The prime reason for this regulation is to ensure that a significant portion of Canadian investments for retirement purposes remain in Canada to serve capital needs for local development. But this restriction flies in the face of the MAI's national treatment and most favoured nation clauses.

Food Security

The production of quality food at fair prices has long been an important dimension of social rights in Canada. Over the past sixty years or so, governments have established significant agricultural support and consumer protection legislation and programs. Although these initiatives left a lot to be desired, they were intended to secure and protect the interests of both the producers and consumers of food. But many of these mechanisms for ensuring food security have come under attack in recent years, starting a trend that would more than likely be accelerated by the ratification of the MAI.

A prime example is Canada's unique system of agriculture supply management for eggs, poultry, and dairy products. The system was designed to benefit both farmers (by providing a stable formula for production costs and thereby guaranteeing regular returns) and consumers (by preventing over-production and guaranteeing quality products). Yet, agribusiness corporations in the U.S. and elsewhere have steadfastly opposed this kind of government intervention in agricultural markets. As a result, Washington has taken repeated action under both NAFTA and the GATT to outlaw Canada's food supply management system, by declaring it to be, among other things, an unfair trade subsidy. Under the WTO's mandate to further liberalize agricultural trade, Ottawa will face increasing pressure to significantly reduce its remaining agricultural tariffs and dismantle much of Canada's supply management system. If the tariff reductions negotiated in the next round of the WTO agricultural talks are sufficient to give agribusiness corporations access to the Canadian market, the MAI tools could be used to open up our food production system to foreign investors. In this context, various federal subsidy programs earmarked for marketing boards could also be targeted as a violation of the MAI's national treatment rules on subsidies. Moreover, agribusiness corporations could challenge any provincial restrictions on the foreign ownership of agricultural lands.

There is also the danger that the MAI's ban on establishing performance standards for foreign corporations could be used to reinforce the WTO's efforts to harmonize worldwide food quality standards through negotiations within what is known as Codex Alimentarius. As the standard-setting agency of the UN Food and Agricultural Organization, Codex Alimentarius is largely controlled by the big food and agribusiness corporations. At Codex, Nestlé is said to have more personnel on different government delegations than there are on any one government delegation. The U.S. delegation at Codex meetings is often dominated by a battery of advisors from General Mills, Kraft, Purina, PepsiCo, Coca-Cola, and a host of other name-brand food industry giants. Armed with MAI restrictions on performance requirements, these corporations would be in a position to ensure that no national government could demand food quality standards that are higher than the international standards they themselves had set as part of Codex.

Meanwhile, manoeuvrings by trade organizations are also affecting Ottawa's commitment to scientific food research and inspection of food products. At the WTO, for example, the Australian government has proposed that responsibilities for food inspection be handed over to corporations. For Canada this would mean that instead of having Ottawa's impartial team of meat inspectors assess the quality of beef imports, corporations involved in the meat industry could do this themselves. As a step in this direction, Ottawa has announced that it is mothballing research dealing with toxins and food contaminants. Instead, Health Canada's food directorate will rely more on studies done by chemical and drug companies, universities, and other countries.

The proposed MAI rules would also give biotechnology corporations added ammunition as they lobby governments to accept new developments in genetic engineering. For example, as described in chapter four, chemical and pharmaceutical giants like Monsanto and Eli Lilly have spent millions of dollars lobbying the Ottawa bureaucracy to permit the use in Canada of bovine growth hormone, a drug known to have negative health effects. These corporations could conceivably make use of the MAI's investor-state mechanisms to challenge the government's ban and claim damages for lost investment opportunities (i.e., expropriation without compensation). Moreover, if a future government with a clear commitment to sustainable agriculture were to introduce legislation to support small and medium-sized farm operations, agribusiness giants like Cargill and Archer Daniels Midland could make effective use of the national treatment clause affecting government subsidies.

Public Services

In addition to health, education, and social services, people need equal access to fire protection, public transportation, water resources, police protection, electrical utilities, waste disposal, library resources, and a wide range of other community services. For the most part, these services are delivered by municipal governments, which, like their federal and provincial counterparts, would also be subject to the rules and disciplines of the MAI.

In Canada, massive cuts in federal social transfer payments are being downloaded not only to the provinces but also to municipal governments, where the real crunch is being felt. Cash-starved municipal governments have begun to contract out public services to private companies. Under the MAI, once a government contracted out a public service like fire protection, bus transportation, garbage pickup, or sewage disposal, it would have to follow the rules for privatization. All municipal government service contracts that required local hiring and content could be challenged for violating the MAI restrictions on performance requirements. Indeed, to avoid costly litigation, municipal governments might be inclined to give preference to foreign companies over domestic or local enterprises. And once a service is privatized, a municipal government would be unable to reclaim it as a public service in better economic times without incurring penalties.

Nor could a government at any level introduce a new public service that would conflict with the disciplines of the MAI. Take, for instance, child care. Since the Royal Commission on the Status of Women in 1970, subsequent royal commissions and task forces have called upon the federal government to create a public, universally accessible, affordable, quality child care program. But if a future federal government were to establish and deliver a publicly funded child care program through community-based non-profit facilities, it could be stopped in its tracks. As noted earlier, delivery of public services through non-profit agencies is considered a subsidy to the private sector under the MAI and therefore subject to the national treatment rules. As long as there are transnational companies that make a business out of providing child care services, the new MAI rules would allow them to demand equal access to government subsidies.

For Ottawa and the provinces to maintain existing public services, let alone adopt new ones like a national child care program, additional public revenues are required. Yet Ottawa's ability to raise new public revenues has been hampered by changes in the tax system, especially the lowering of corporate taxes, as well as by monetary policies based on high interest rates. Since the Mulroney government's tax reforms of the 1980s, the percentage of overall federal revenues contributed through corporate taxes dropped from 15 to as low as 5 percent, the lowest rate among the G-7 countries. In 1994 alone, more than 80,000 corporations making profits in this country ended up paying no income taxes at all, due to numerous tax loopholes and write-offs.

The MAI could eventually make the problem of low tax revenues even worse. For now, the proposed MAI rules will not apply to taxation. Yet, the very fact that corporate taxation has been identified as a form of "creeping expropriation" may be a portent of things to come. Although the MAI negotiators plan to take more time to study how corporate taxation may be included in the new global investment rules, it is clear that they have already begun to hinder public revenue generation by forbidding governments to use taxes to control capital outflows or the repatriation of profits. Given these constraints, there is little chance that Ottawa will be in a position to defend, let alone promote and expand, the social rights of its citizens.

SIX

THE WAR ON CULTURAL RIGHTS

*"The prospect of pain must be inserted into the equation,
else the solution will never be suitable."*
— JACK VALENTI, PRESIDENT, U.S. MOTION PICTURE ASSOCIATION

More than any other issue in the Canadian political landscape, culture is a direct expression of who we are as people and as a country. And as part of our economy, it is especially vulnerable to the ravages of global investment treaties. The proponents of economic globalization argue that Canada must abandon its historic policies of cultural protectionism and content regulation; culture, in their view, should be an export commodity like any other, subject to competition in an open market. But to expose our cultural industries to that market, especially if the MAI is ratified, is to risk losing sight of our identity as Canadians; in effect, we would be putting our uniqueness up for sale.

Canada's Cultural Heritage

From the mid-1930s until recently, successive Canadian governments designed and implemented cultural policies for at least
two main reasons: to build a strong and dynamic pool of
Canadian artistic talent and cultural enterprises; and to ensure
that Canadians' own stories were told and our values and history preserved. These policies were created first and foremost to
serve Canadians, not to serve an international trade agenda.
Living next to the biggest superpower in the world, our ancestors
knew they had to carve out a space for our unique Canadian
perspective. Public support for Canadian culture has been crucial to our survival as a nation.

As the Canadian Conference of the Arts (CCA) explains,
"Some [cultural policies] have been designed to ensure fair competition in the Canadian market between Canada's cultural
producers and those who enjoy enormous economies of scale as
a result of producing for a primary market many times the size
of our own. Others assist the cultural industries in meeting the
challenge of distributing cultural products across Canada's enormous geographical distances."

Promotion of Canadian culture takes three forms: subsidies,
investment polices, and Canadian content quotas. Broadcasting
policy includes content regulations in radio (30 percent of all
music played must be Canadian) and content regulations in television (60 percent of each day's schedule and at least 50 percent
of prime time programming must be Canadian); tax breaks for
businesses advertising on Canadian broadcast stations; subsidies
of new talent through a program called FACTOR/Music Action;
and investment controls limiting non-Canadian investment in
broadcasting, telecommunications, and cable companies to no
more than one-third of voting shares and requiring Canadian

control in all cases. As well, the federal government funds the CBC (to the tune of approximately $800 million in 1997).

Television production is regulated by Canadian content rules and Canadian Radio-Television and Telecommunications Commission (CRTC) conditions of licence, as well as by international co-production treaties concluded with more than forty other nations; it is funded by the Canadian Television and Cable Production Fund, and a tax credit for a portion of labour costs incurred by Canadian television and film producers.

Film production is promoted by Telefilm Canada; the National Film Board; and by regulations requiring that certain television services broadcast a minimum number of Canadian movies.

Book publishing is supported by the Book Publishing Industry Development Program, providing direct subsidies to Canadian publishers according to sales of Canadian titles; a Publications Distribution Assistance Program (scheduled for elimination in 1998); and investment controls limiting the amount of foreign control over Canadian publishing companies.

Magazine publishing has flourished under the protection of postal subsidies (greatly reduced in recent budgets); tax breaks for businesses advertising in Canadian magazines; and a prohibition on "split-run" editions of U.S. magazines that insert a token amount of Canadian content in order to sell ads in Canada.

The Canadian government also supports the Canada Council, which administers $90 million each year in grants to the cultural sector; administers the Federal Business Development Bank, which grants loans to a small number of firms in the cultural sector; uses the Income Tax Act to maintain control of newspapers in Canadian hands; and funds the National Arts Centre, the National Gallery, the National Archives, the National Library, and a number of museums, including the Canadian Museum of Civilization.

These policies and institutions have produced a lively and vibrant cultural heritage in Canada and have created a springboard for Canadian artists on the world stage, in spite of the continued domination of Canada by American culture. Canada's arts and cultural industries are intrinsic to our sense of nation, to the cultivation of a shared identity, and to a prosperous economy.

Internal Assault

In the 1990s, however, every cultural institution and sector is at risk. Seismic changes in Canadian society and international relations have created unforeseen challenges to the very existence of Canadian cultural policies and institutions, which, says *The Globe and Mail*'s Doug Saunders, "are increasingly forced to balance their responsibility to Canadian audiences against the demands of lucrative foreign buyers."

As well, the free market ideology that drove the Conservative Party under Brian Mulroney is now firmly rooted in the current economic ministers and senior bureaucrats of the federal Liberal government and in the political advisors to Jean Chrétien himself. The tendency of both these governments has been to shift away from policies and regulations that promote a vibrant domestic cultural industry to an emphasis on advancing the export potential of individual artists and products. Chrétien's Liberals openly favour the latter over maintaining content rules to protect a distinctly Canadian voice for Canadians.

As a consequence, federal funding for culture has been dramatically reduced in the last decade. The assault has been relentless. In the late 1980s, the government replaced the Federal Sales Tax with the GST and eliminated the exemption for books, magazines, and newspapers. Those sectors were hit hard: more than one hundred magazine titles have disappeared since 1991.

Then the public broadcaster was hit. Measured in constant dollars (that is, excluding inflation), funding to the CBC has declined by 47 percent in a decade, and its workforce has been cut in half. Funding for the Canada Council, the National Film Board, and the National Library and Museums was slashed by 30 percent in the infamous 1995 Martin budget alone. Between 1990 and 1992, most indirect forms of support — tax credits and other incentives to attract investment in publishing, recording, and films — dropped from almost $1 billion to zero. Communications analyst Paul Audley reports a 41 percent reduction in overall federal spending on culture (indirect and direct funding combined) between 1989 and 1996.

The Canadian advertising industry was bought out almost entirely by American giants in the early 1990s. The Canadian book industry is fighting to ward off the huge U.S. bookselling chains and the ten or so giant book publishers that threaten to dominate the industry and control which books get to market. As it is, continent-wide book distribution makes it difficult to justify the production and promotion of titles only of interest to Canadians.

Meanwhile, a handful of powerful private corporations are expanding their control over the media. Conrad Black's Hollinger Inc. now owns or controls sixty of Canada's 105 daily newspapers, including 80 percent of all the papers in Ontario and all the dailies in Saskatchewan, Newfoundland, and Prince Edward Island. Just ten corporations control 55 percent of revenues in radio, an increase of 50 percent over the past decade. Three giant cable companies have nearly 70 percent of the TV market. This trend in Canada mirrors the global trend in which a handful of players like Ted Turner, Disney, Time Warner, and Berlusconi control not only the major entertainment outlets, but the news as well. These corporate powerhouses are pressing politicians everywhere to eliminate public broadcasting and remove the civic purpose mandate of TV, perhaps the most powerful medium on earth. They also want national foreign ownership rules to to be lifted.

Izzy Asper, president of CanWest Global Communications, would hurry their entry into Canada. In a January 1995 letter to Heritage Canada, he proposed that foreign investors be allowed 49.9 percent ownership of Canadian broadcasting companies and unlimited access to non-voting shares. *The Financial Post* said the Canadian Association of Broadcasters "didn't oppose" the suggestion.

Many in the Canadian film and television industries now seek international partners for their productions, but in order to sell them in other countries, the final products cannot be overtly Canadian. An export boom has resulted in a proliferation of independent Canadian companies whose American offices now dominate their business and artistic operations. *The Globe and Mail* reports that the Canadian government agencies that finance broadcast media now tend to operate like banks, looking more favourably on these international (less Canadian) projects.

Former Liberal trade minister Art Eggleton set off a firestorm of protest in early 1997 when he openly differed with heritage minister Sheila Copps on the future of Canadian culture in a global economy. "The trend to open markets and communications," he said, "is global and irreversible."

His position is reminiscent of Mulroney's finance minister, Michael Wilson, who, in 1991, overruled then culture minister Marcel Masse on policy intended to Canadianize the book publishing industry. In both cases, it is clear that power over culture resides not with the minister responsible in name, but with the real power brokers in government: the ministers and bureaucrats responsible for trade and finance.

This has been confirmed again in the very delicate negotiations on how culture would be treated in the MAI. Heritage minister Sheila Copps's office has confirmed that neither the minister nor her staff is party to the talks, which are being handled exclusively by Foreign Affairs. Janet Bax, director of communications for Heritage Canada, says this is mainly because "for us to be making any comments now could jeopardize our negotiating position."

Eggleton isn't the only influential insider set to destroy Canada's cultural protections. In fact, the forces of privatization are now operating inside the very institutions whose core mandate is the promotion of Canadian culture. James McCoubrey, the new executive vice-president of the CBC, spent most of his career with the huge transnational advertising firm, Young and Rubicam, and is, in the words of *The Globe and Mail,* "pure private sector." Françoise Bertrand, who in 1996 replaced Keith Spicer as chair of the CRTC, sees her role as strengthening the cultural sector before it is fully deregulated — a scenario she says is inevitable. She insists that under her stewardship, not only her job, but also Canadian content regulations, will disappear. "It will. We know that."

In April 1997 the Senate's Standing Committee on Transport and Communications published a shocking report, *Wired to Win: Canada's International Competitive Position in Communications,* calling for the dismantling of Canada's cultural policies in favour of open global competition. "To strengthen Canadian firms abroad, it is necessary to create a competitive domestic marketplace that is turned aggressively outwards to foreign markets . . .

Clearly, commercial and trade policies must get in step with new technologies and market forces . . . If Canada wishes to increase its exports of services and products in the communications sector, it will have to open its domestic market to foreign services and products . . . A possible solution would be to move away from policies based on protection and towards those that seek more pro-actively to *promote* Canadian products — both at home and abroad."

External Assault

This change in the position of the Canadian government regarding culture is no doubt music to the ears of the U.S. entertainment industry, America's biggest export and a major proponent of the MAI.

From the early days of film and television, the U.S. sought to use the GATT to achieve the unimpeded export of its entertainment products to certain other countries, including Canada, that were attempting to provide some space for their own artists and industry by establishing conditions on American imports. In 1985, American entertainment, recording, and publishing industry executives, polled by CBS, singled out Canadian cultural policies as major impediments to their global commercial activities and called for trade rules to bring their neighbour into line.

Culture was a very contentious issue in both the FTA and NAFTA negotiations. The Mulroney Tories claimed that they negotiated full protection for Canadian culture with an exemption for cultural industries and policies. They said less about the price they had to pay to get it. The exemption in both trade agreements is subject to the notorious "notwithstanding" clause that says if Canada invokes the cultural exemption, the U.S. can retaliate with measures of "equivalent commercial effect" and do so using sectors unrelated to culture. Ivan Bernier, a trade expert with the faculty of law at Laval University, explains, "What Article 2005 [of NAFTA] says, in reality, is that if a Party is ready to pay the price, it can maintain cultural measures that are incompatible with the Agreement."

Mel Clark, deputy trade negotiator of the Tokyo round of the GATT, adds, "While one article exempts the cultural industry from the agreement, another puts culture right back in by giving the U.S. the right to retaliate against Canada for 'actions' the U.S. deems 'inconsistent' with it. Yet another article permits the U.S. to circumvent the dispute settlement procedure when it retaliates. This means that the U.S. has the legal right to unilaterally decide if a Canadian cultural measure is 'inconsistent' with the NAFTA, to retaliate against Canada, and to select the nature and severity of the retaliation. The U.S. is the accuser, the umpire and the enforcer."

During the free trade talks, the Canadian government argued that the U.S. always had the right to punish Canadian policies and that trade-based rules would be an improvement. Section 301 of an American law, the U.S. Trade Expansion Act, gives the U.S. the right to unilaterally retaliate against the companies of GATT partners operating in the U.S. if it deems that a (totally legal) practice of that country is negatively affecting U.S. commercial interests.

However, as Paul Audley notes, at least this punishment was meted out unilaterally, without the formal approbation of other trade partners or the "offending country" itself. By signing the FTA and NAFTA, "Canada recognized and accepted a new U.S. right — the right to hit back if Canada took any cultural measures inconsistent with free trade principles." If Canada's right to maintain cultural policies is so self-evident, Audley asks, "why had we given a blanket approval in advance to U.S. retaliation?" In any case, the U.S. maintains the right of unilateral retaliation.

U.S. reaction to the cultural exemption was mixed. FTA trade negotiator Peter Murphy called it a "joke" and said he had used Canadian concerns over culture as a bargaining tool to gain other concessions. U.S. Motion Picture Association president Jack Valenti called it "Armageddon time" and declared war on it. But the American government knew that it set a precedent that could be troublesome in GATT talks; in its legislation implementing the FTA, it bound future administrations to seek elimination of the exemption.

In 1995, the NAFTA cultural exemption came to the test when Canada dropped a U.S. country music channel from cable TV in order to enforce its long-standing policy of giving preferential treatment to domestic specialty TV channels. The U.S. trade representative at the time, Mickey Kantor, issued threats of massive retaliation, and called for the elimination of key Canadian content provisions of the CRTC. Canadian officials capitulated and came up with a last-minute compromise that avoided a trade war. But the U.S. was prepared for action. Said an executive of Westinghouse (co-owner of the American station), "The trigger [was] on the gun and [the Americans were] not concerned about using it."

That same year, Canadian cultural groups came into possession of a secret U.S. document outlining a global strategy to eliminate the cultural exemption clause in NAFTA and ensure no similar provisions would be included in future trade deals. Said Keith Kelly of the Canadian Conference of the Arts, "This is a part of a series of very orchestrated moves by the Americans to advance their mass entertainment business, not only in Canada but around the world." No wonder Art Eggleton, when he was still trade minister, was blunt. "We don't have any cultural protections under NAFTA. That's a myth. We never did."

In any case, regional agreements like NAFTA are only allowed if they are in full compliance with the GATT. Whatever limited exemptions Canada received for culture in the continental trade deals are wiped out in the larger jurisdiction of the WTO.

There are only two articles in the GATT that refer to cultural goods: the first, a weak provision subject to negotiation for elimination, allows limited screen quotas of domestic films; the second provides some protection for national treasures of artistic, historic, or archaeological value. Aside from these, all cultural products are subject to GATT rules, including the rule of national treatment, so that cultural industries of other signatory countries must be given the same benefits as Canadian companies.

When the World Trade Organization came into being in 1994, it included no exclusion for culture. The issue had become so sensitive that it was put aside for future discussions. As Audley notes, whereas the FTA and NAFTA gave Canada the right to act and the U.S. the right to react with respect to culture, the WTO simply prevents Canada from acting in its cultural interests at all. There is no acknowledgement that culture is special in the WTO; it is simply another commodity, like any widget.

It should come as no surprise, then, that when the U.S. decided to challenge Canada's protection of its magazine industry, it chose to lay a complaint under the WTO, and not NAFTA. The U.S. argued that Canada's policies violated the national treatment provisions of the WTO by giving preferential treatment to its own magazines.

In July 1997, Canada lost, on appeal, its key policies to protect its magazine industry: the 80 percent tariff and excise tax on split-runs and postal subsidies for Canadian magazines. Magazines were ruled "a product" and their country of origin was deemed irrelevant. An official with Heritage Canada concedes, "It's outrageous . . . They're saying a magazine is a magazine, no matter whether it is Canadian or American."

The decision is final. The Canadian government announced it would fully comply; its only alternative is to accept trade retaliation of equal commercial value, which would pit culture against other interests and sectors of Canadian society.

The loss was greater than the Canadian government feared and was greeted with deep consternation by the entire cultural sector in Canada. Canadian and American trade experts all agreed this was a precedent-setting decision with far-reaching implications for other cultural policies. U.S. trade representative Charlene Barshefsky was jubilant, saying the decision would serve as a useful weapon against other Canadian cultural practices.

The Globe and Mail called the decision a "severe blow" to Canada's right to protect its cultural sector from Americanization. *The Ottawa Citizen* said the decision was an attack "on the very foundations of federal policy underpinning the survival of popular Canadian magazines such as *Maclean's* and *Saturday Night*" and "may carry disastrous implications for Canadian culture . . . The latest judgement may make other Canadian content laws such as the ones for broadcast media vulnerable to foreign assault."

The ruling has left Canadian cultural policy in legal limbo. This is the fragile state of Canadian culture as Canada negotiates the MAI.

MAI Assault

The MAI represents a lethal attack on what remains of all three forms of cultural protection in Canada: subsidies, Canadian content quotas, and, most particularly, investment rules. The Business and Industry Advisory Group to the OECD, which includes Canadian representatives, has advised the OECD to oppose any "cultural carve-out" for the MAI. No cultural sector or practice, not even national treasures, would be included in the general "sovereignty" exceptions to investor protection in the proposed draft of the MAI.

On close examination, it becomes clear that the U.S. entertainment industry has carefully and systematically used trade and investment agreements to take apart Canada's cultural regime, piece by piece. An OECD working group anticipates that the MAI would supersede the provisions of earlier trade agreements, including NAFTA's cultural exemption and the weak protections of the GATT.

Canadian government officials insist they are seeking a general exemption in the MAI for culture, a move the U.S. strongly opposes. Having successfully kept culture out of the WTO, the U.S. is hardly likely to put it back into the MAI.

The U.S. insists that if Canada wants to protect its culture, it must seek an individual country-specific reservation. This would allow the Canadian government to save face on this politically sensitive issue and sell the deal to the Canadian public, without even slightly jeopardizing the U.S. position. For country-specific reservations would simply set Canada's cultural policies up as a moving "hit list" which could be picked off one at a time under the non-negotiable clauses of standstill and roll-back.

The standstill clause means that no new policies or protections could replace those that have been negotiated away, abandoned as part of cost-cutting measures, or lost in decisions like the WTO ruling on magazines. As well, any new technology developed for the hardware that delivers culture would not be subject to Canadian content rules on software. The MAI's roll-back provision, however, would place even current policy at risk; it would be used to enforce conformity to open investment rules over any area where culture and investment meet. Over time, roll-back would eliminate any reservations for culture that Canada might acquire temporarily.

Further, the principles of national treatment and most favoured nation would apply to the granting of investment incentives, subsidies, and grants, which could not be restricted on the basis of country of ownership. This goes beyond NAFTA, which explicitly excluded subsidies from national treatment provisions. Andrew Jackson of the Canadian Labour Congress explains, "This provision would mean that cultural subsidies could not be allocated exclusively to Canadian artists, publications, production companies, etc."

Because the MAI would also extend the national treatment and most favoured nation clauses to the privatization of public enterprises, any federal or provincial cultural institution that has been run as a non-profit by government and is now slated for privatization would have to be tendered to the corporations of every country that is a signatory to the treaty. The government in question could not even give Canadian companies the advantage of prior notice, nor could it make special arrangements with Canadian workers or communities to buy the cultural institution or to distribute shares to the general public.

In privatization-crazy Canada, it would be almost impossible to maintain production or content control over institutions that have formed the core of Canadian culture. For instance, if the

MAI is in place when the Harris government moves to privatize TVOntario — as it has promised to do — *it will not be possible to require that production or content control of TVO stay in Ontario or even Canadian hands.*

Magazines

The Canadian magazine industry is fighting for its life in the wake of the WTO ruling. As it is, 80 percent of magazines bought on Canadian newsstands are now foreign, and seven out of ten Canadian magazine titles don't show up on Canadian newsstands at all. The removal of borders for magazine trade would dramatically favour the American industry, which ships $700 million worth of magazines into Canada every year, compared with the only $10 million in exports of Canadian magazines to the U.S.

The giant U.S. media companies like Time Warner are now poised to flood the Canadian market with versions of their mass-market magazines, such as *Time, Sports Illustrated,* and *People.* George Gross, executive vice-president of the Magazine Publishers of America, says the American industry is "waiting to see when they'll be free to get into heightened Canadian activities." The "Canadian" version of these — the split-runs that are now legal in Canada — will bleed advertising dollars from domestic magazines, threatening their survival in the small Canadian market.

Gordon Ritchie, a former deputy minister of industry who helped negotiate the FTA, said, "Having probed the weak spot in the wall and been able to get through, the Americans are going to step up the assault. There's no question that they're on a crusade here. This is the thin edge of the wedge." Canadian ambassador to the U.S. Raymond Chrétien noted with surprise "how widely perceived, distributed, noticed this decision is" in the U.S.

The only remaining protections for Canadian magazines in the wake of the WTO ruling are very costly direct government subsidies to the industry and a tax measure that allows businesses to deduct the cost of advertising in domestic — but not foreign — periodicals. If disputed under the GATT, the former would likely be allowed, and the latter struck down. *However, the MAI's national treatment provisions would prohibit the use of both of these measures unless American magazines were given the same rights and access to the same subsidies.* Canadian trade expert Peter Clark explains, "Anything that treats Canadian magazines differently from foreign magazines is going to run into national treatment problems."

Broadcasting and Film

In a recent report by the U.S. trade representative, the Canadian Broadcasting Act was identified as a barrier to U.S. exports and targeted for elimination. The WTO has scheduled negotiations for the global deregulation of broadcasting for January 1, 2000. Areas for discussion include the definition of broadcasting, ownership and control of broadcast licensees, and "access and reciprocity to domestic and foreign markets." The Canadian government is working with the pro-privatization U.S. government and industry to come up with a "common North American position" to take to the WTO. This process, combined with the MAI, would doom Canada's domestic industry.

All of the policies and practices that protect Canadian broadcasting and films would likely be illegal under the MAI. Canadian content rules would violate MAI national treatment and most favoured nation rules. The MAI clause on performance requirements would mean that a foreign film or broadcasting company would not have to locate in Canada or hire Canadian artists in order to operate here and receive the going subsidies and tax breaks. And these companies would be free to take 100 percent of their profits out of Canada. Parliamentary subsidies to the CBC, the Canada Council, and the National Film Board could be challenged.

The government could no longer require radio stations to play Canadian music, television to air Canadian programs, or film companies to produce Canadian material to qualify for grants and tax breaks. In fact, all tax breaks would have to be granted equally to the entertainment corporations of all the OECD countries (and eventually, to the 182 countries of the WTO as well), or cancelled. The CBC could not be treated differently than ABC, CNN, CBS, NBC, and their counterparts in the other OECD countries.

The MAI would also prohibit simulcasting, the process in which Canadian viewers watching a U.S. show on a U.S. channel receive a cable signal that switches the show to the Canadian channel with the broadcast rights, so that viewers see Canadian instead of American commercials. Bill C-58, the income tax law that makes it advantageous for Canadian companies to advertise on Canadian stations, could also be challenged under the MAI.

The Canadian government could no longer restrict foreign film companies from granting Canadian distribution rights for their independently made movies to the Dutch entertainment giant, Polygram; as a result, Canadian distributors could quickly be shut out of this lucrative business.

The business community is ready. Several telecommunications giants testified before the Senate committee hearings on the future of broadcasting and film in Canada (the hearings that produced *Wired to Win*) and found Senate members to be a receptive audience. The corporations' recommendations foretell the future for Canadian broadcasting and film under the MAI:

> IBM Canada recommended a three-phase transition period that would, within a period of roughly 10 years, see the complete phasing out of all regulations in the area of licensing, foreign ownership, Canadian content, and mandatory contributions to Canadian production . . . The final phase would see the lifting of all rules: unconditional exemptions, 100 per cent foreign ownership, no content rules, and no mandatory expenditure on Canadian production.

Publishing

Canada's fragile book publishing industry could be greatly affected by the MAI. The Book Publishing Industry Development ment Program would have to be open to foreign publishers or cancelled, as would the $3 million the federal government allocates annually to Canadian publishers for book distribution and marketing. Investment controls whereby foreign firms may not establish new undertakings in the book trade, nor acquire a majority of any Canadian company, would violate MAI national treatment and most favoured nation provisions. Nor could Canada continue to require that an indirect acquisition by a foreign firm of a Canadian publishing subsidiary of another foreign firm be "of net benefit" to Canada.

Under the MAI, a U.S. book publishing giant could buy up a major Canadian publisher and refuse to produce any creative works by Canadians, but still qualify for industrial incentives offered by the Canadian government. Book distribution would be open to continental competition, as would bookstores. There would be no stopping the entry into Canada of the several giant American book chains that have closed down independent stores all over the U.S. There would be no way to force foreign publishing, distribution, and book companies operating in Canada to employ Canadians, in either the arts or business end of the industry.

The audience for all books would now be North American; under the economies of scale of a continental industry, Canadian writers would have to appeal to an American audience in order to be published. The book you are reading now might not find a publisher in a post-MAI jurisdiction that allowed no policy to promote books written for and about Canada.

Copyright

Canada's new Copyright Act provides a series of what the Canadian Conference of the Arts calls "economic and moral rights" to the creators and owners of intellectual property. Among other things, the act provides compensation to Canadian musicians and producers for radio airplay, and maintains a fund from a tax on sales of blank cassette tapes to compensate Canadian performers and producers for the home copying that deprives them of royalties.

The U.S. has placed Canada on a "watch list" for possible trade violations arising from the Copyright Act. The watch list is the first step to launching a full-scale trade dispute. Charlene Barshefsky says her government is "very, very concerned" about it. "This is a violation of national treatment, among other violations, and we are looking at the possibility of bringing a case on that matter."

The Canadian government claims it has a defence for copyright under NAFTA and the GATT, although the language they are relying on is ambiguous at best. But the government would not have a leg to stand on after ratification of the MAI; under the national treatment and most favoured nation rules, and the ban on performance requirements, the artists and producers of American and other OECD countries would have to be given equal access to any compensation funds or Canada would be in clear violation of its treaty obligations. The MAI would kill Canadian copyright before it ever had a chance to work.

Newspapers

Canada's magazine industry was not the only sector to be negatively affected by the recent WTO ruling. Canadian newspapers also lost the right to preferential postal rates. Now, the only remaining support for Canada's newspapers is a provision of the Income Tax Act that restricts foreign ownership by allowing businesses to deduct 100 percent of their advertising costs only if they advertise in Canadian publications. Because this practice puts foreign publications at a distinct disadvantage in attracting advertising revenues, it would clearly be illegal under the MAI.

A senior federal official admitted in May 1997 that the MAI would lead to the elimination of all foreign ownership restrictions, including those that protect newspapers. The assistant deputy minister of heritage, Michael Binder, told *The Globe and Mail* that the government would "absolutely have to revise" the four-year-old Telecommunications Act, which contains restrictions limiting foreign ownership in the telecommunications sector. Similarly, ratifying the MAI would mean opening the door to foreign media corporations. Canada would find itself out of the Conrad Black frying pan and into the Rupert Murdoch fire.

The threat to Canadian culture by the proposed MAI, with its twenty-year lock-in, cannot be overstated. If Canada endorses this treaty, a vibrant domestic industry, with its Canadian perspective on the arts, news, and history, may be lost, perhaps forever.

SEVEN

THE ECLIPSE OF POLITICAL RIGHTS

*"It is only by decentralizing the state even more
that we can obtain more efficient public services and a
reduction in deficits. We should give the power
to spend to those who have little power to borrow."*
— ANDRÉ BÉRARD, CEO, NATIONAL BANK OF CANADA

One of the central features of
democracy is the right of citizens to participate in decisions
affecting their lives. In principle, all citizens should be involved
in shaping their own economic, social, cultural, and ecological
futures. In the same way, each nation of people should have the
right to political self-determination; that is, to carve out its own
economic, social, cultural, and ecological destiny. While these
political rights are, to a certain extent, enshrined in the UN's
Universal Declaration of Human Rights and its accompanying
Covenants, they are increasingly being eclipsed by new global
economic forces like the MAI.

In most democratic societies, the political rights of citizens and the nation-state itself are reflected in a constitution. Although written using complex legal jargon, a constitution is supposed to outline the basic rules by which a nation of people governs itself. It is in the constitution of a nation-state that the division of powers between the various branches of government is laid out along with corresponding responsibilities and areas of authority. It is also through a nation's constitution that we get a glimpse of the extent to which the political, participatory rights of citizens are both recognized and protected.

Canadians are certainly no strangers to constitutional debate. Indeed, in the eyes of the rest of the world, constitutional squabbles appear to be a favourite political pastime in Canada. In just over a decade and a half, Canadians have gone head-to-head with one another in battles over the repatriation of the Constitution in 1982, the Meech Lake Accord in the late 1980s, and the Charlottetown Accord in 1992. While for the most part these battles were focused on an internal struggle over the political future of Quebec and its relationship with the rest of the country, there have been *external* forces at work redesigning the Canadian federation and redefining the political rights of Canadians with little or no public discussion and debate.

As constitutional lawyer David Schneiderman reminds us, the Canadian approach to democratic government differs significantly from that of the United States. Following British constitutional tradition, Canada has been a parliamentary democracy in which elected legislators have considerable powers. Under the British constitution, Parliament has the authority and power "to make and unmake any law whatsoever." In the Canadian constitutional regime, this legislative power was divided between two levels of government, federal and provincial, in order to avoid the abuses of centralized political authority.

Citing examples of how creative social policy in Canada has been initiated by both federal and provincial governments, Schneiderman argues that this Canadian model of federalism has proven in the past to be both democratic and energetic.

But in the new global economy, says Schneiderman, Canada's democratic model of "energetic federalism" is being "drawn further into the American constitutional orbit." As noted earlier (see chapter two), trade and investment regimes like NAFTA, the WTO, and the MAI have been grounded in U.S. constitutional principles and law, especially with regard to the protection of private property and due process through the courts. In the past, the Canadian Parliament and provincial legislatures had the legislative authority and power to make decisions about the regulation of private property and the economy in general. Under the new trade and investment regimes, Canadian legislators are now seriously constrained in their power to act on these crucial aspects of public policy, and find themselves increasingly compelled to follow U.S. constitutional law and procedure.

As Schneiderman contends, NAFTA has already introduced a "new legal discourse" by entitling investors to pursue American-style constitutional remedies. A case in point is the dispute over Ottawa's proposed legislation on plain cigarette packaging. In 1994–5, the major U.S. tobacco companies threatened to sue the Canadian government for "hundreds of millions of dollars" if it went ahead with the legislation. Legal opinions were first commissioned from former U.S. trade ambassador Carla Hills, who argued on behalf of the tobacco giants that a law requiring plain packaging would be a violation of the NAFTA takings rule because it constituted a ban against cigarette advertising. But when the related case known as *RJR-MacDonald* went to the Supreme Court of Canada, it was the Canadian Charter of Rights and Freedoms that was invoked to declare that a ban on promotional advertising and a requirement for unattributed mandatory health warnings (which amount to plain packaging) were unjustifiable restrictions on "the freedom of expression." The *RJR-MacDonald* ruling, says Schneiderman, "suggests that the Charter accomplishes some of the same ends as NAFTA's takings clause."

Initially incorporated into the Canadian Constitution at the time of its repatriation in 1982, the Charter of Rights and Freedoms allows citizens to defend their civil and democratic rights through the courts. But the Charter has been most effectively used by big business to protect its property rights. Notes University of Toronto law professor Michael Mandel, the Charter has become "a potent symbol" in "transforming business rights into moral rights."

It is through this new legal discourse, says Schneiderman, that the operational framework of the Canadian Constitution is gradually being transformed from one espousing "energetic federalism" to one promoting more "limited government." Instead of addressing economic affairs through legislative action in the parliamentary tradition, Ottawa and the provinces appear to have become increasingly dependent on developing economic policies in the framework of U.S. property rights principles, obliged as they are to defend these policies through dispute settlement panels and courts that are driven by U.S. takings laws.

The consequence of this change of focus is that the political rights of corporations are enhanced, while the political rights of governments, let alone their citizens, are diminished. The proposed MAI would, of course, reinforce this trend in spades. Not only has the MAI been designed on the basis of U.S. property law and takings rules, but the investor-state dispute mechanisms would allow transnational corporations to use the courts to force

Ottawa and the provinces to conform with American constitutional principles when it comes to regulating the economy and related social, cultural, and environmental matters. Since the MAI would be an international treaty, it would supersede laws created by elected members of Parliament and provincial legislatures. But it might further prove to be a dynamic constitutional force, if the government finds it necessary to amend the Constitution to make it compatible with MAI rules. In fact, the Chrétien government has already set the stage for massive changes in Canadian federalism to coincide with the new global investment and trade regimes. Although these changes have profound constitutional implications, they are quietly taking place with little or no public discussion and debate.

Market Federalism

A prime example of a change made to Canadian federalism with little fanfare is the so-called Agreement on Internal Trade (AIT) between Ottawa and the provinces, signed in June of 1994. The AIT was intended to eliminate trade barriers between the provinces and create a free market union that would complement Canada's external commitments under the FTA, NAFTA, and, increasingly, the WTO. But in so doing, the AIT gave Ottawa sweeping powers to impose "free market disciplines" and "corporate-friendly policies" on all political jurisdictions in Canada. More specifically, the federal implementing legislation for the AIT authorizes the federal cabinet to "suspend rights or privileges granted by the Government of Canada to the provinces under the Agreement or any federal law . . . to modify or suspend the application of any federal law with respect to the provinces . . . [and] to take any other measures" considered necessary to enforce these disciplines.

What this means, in effect, is that U.S. constitutional principles regarding free markets, property rights, and economic regulation are being woven into the fabric of Canadian federalism through the AIT. Any provincial policy or legislation designed to implement certain labour, environmental, cultural, or even local hiring priorities that are perceived to conflict with the spirit and disciplines of the AIT could be targeted by Ottawa or a corporation and struck down. The upshot is that the AIT significantly alters the face of Canadian federalism by giving Ottawa the clout to punish provinces that are not following free market disciplines or corporate-friendly policies. And this remaking of the Canadian federation, in turn, readies Canada for participation in a world governed by global investment rules under the MAI.

In short, the AIT constitutes the elements of a market-driven form of federalism, dreamed of by Ottawa politicians and bureaucrats and ardently pursued and shaped by the representatives of big business. When Liberal MP Raymond Chan, now Secretary of State for the Asia-Pacific Rim, introduced the AIT bill in Parliament, he declared that "the government has felt strong and repeated pressure from the private sector" to bring forth the AIT. Chan then went on to name what amounted to the sponsoring agents of the AIT, including the Business Council on National Issues, the Canadian Manufacturers' Association, the Canadian Chamber of Commerce, the Canadian Federation of Independent Business, the Canadian Bankers Association, and the Canadian Construction Association.

To make matters worse, the Chrétien government has also tried to reinforce this kind of market federalism by introducing a Regulatory Efficiency Act. The proposed legislation would give corporations the right to bypass health, safety, and environmental regulations. Cabinet ministers and government bureaucrats, rather than Parliament itself, would have the power to grant companies dispensations from specific pieces of regulatory legislation. And these ministers and bureaucrats would have no obligation to inform the public of any intention to grant dispensation to a particular corporation. In effect, the proposed act would abrogate a 300-year-old British parliamentary tradition that maintained that, under the Bill of Rights, only the House of Commons and not the Crown could exercise powers of dispensation.

The proposed Regulatory Efficiency Act would also go a long way towards enforcing the rules and disciplines of the MAI, by giving transnational corporations some buttons to push when they want to bypass Parliament to gain exemptions from any regulatory measures. Undoubtedly, this is why BCNI chief Tom d'Aquino has repeatedly urged the Chrétien government to ignore the bill's "fearmongering" opponents and get on with the task of ensuring a speedy passage. No less than three versions of the bill have been introduced over the past two years, and since the Chrétien government still appears determined to give ministers powers to grant regulatory exemptions to corporations, it is quite likely that a new bill will be tabled in the next parliamentary session.

The Big Business Agenda

The new market federalism is not only a product of the Ottawa politicians and bureaucrats; the real architects are the powerful representatives of Canada's big business interests. During the constitutional forums initiated by the Mulroney government leading up to the Charlottetown Accord, the BCNI vigorously advocated a revamping of the federation around the theme of a "common market" and "economic union." Prominent among their initial proposals was the entrenchment of property rights as an operating principle of the Canadian Constitution. Although the big business agenda was temporarily stalled by the Charlottetown process, the campaign continued.

Since Charlottetown, the BCNI has sponsored numerous conferences calling for a more decentralized Canada and advocating a radical reorganization of federal and provincial powers. According to the BCNI's model of federalism, Ottawa should have exclusive powers over fiscal and monetary policy, international trade, and national defence, all of which are crucial for favourable conditions for profitable and secure investment. The remaining state powers and responsibilities should be decentralized. Mining, forestry, tourism, and housing, says the BCNI, should go to the provinces along with regional development, municipal affairs, recreation, and sports. The provinces should also take over responsibilities for fisheries, agriculture, environment, culture, communication, industry, and export promotion, as well as labour training, social housing, child care, and student loans.

At one level, the BCNI argues that this highly decentralized model of federalism is the key to holding the country together. With another Quebec referendum on the horizon, the BCNI claims that a full-scale decentralization of federal powers will not only give Quebec what it wants and needs to maintain control over its own culture and society, but will also serve to placate other power-hungry provinces. Indeed, during the summer of 1997 the Business Council even saw fit to bypass the prime minister and go straight to the nine pro-Canada premiers, urging them to take leadership on the national unity issue. By encouraging Alberta's Ralph Klein to take the lead, the BCNI hoped a strong case for a decentralized federation would bring soft nationalists in Quebec onside. Although the plan faltered, it revealed how the BCNI is prepared to wield its power behind the scenes to restructure the Canadian federation without formal constitutional change, let alone public discussion and debate.

Yet, a decentralized, market-driven federation is hardly the answer to Canada's political woes as a nation-state. Canada is already one of the most decentralized federations in the world. Becoming even more balkanized, politically as well as economically, does not seem like much of a recipe for national unity. But the real objective behind the BCNI agenda is to make the Canadian federation more compatible with the new global trade and investment regimes. By consolidating Ottawa's powers over macro-economic policy, the national government can do what big business wants it to do, namely, create a favourable climate for transnational investment and competition. By downloading its powers and responsibilities for programs and services to the provinces, Ottawa is no longer obligated to provide and maintain national standards. It is much easier for corporations to deal directly with the provinces, playing one against another, than to be restricted by national rules and standards set by Ottawa. In addition, a decentralized, market-driven federation would certainly be much more compatible with the trade rules and ideology of the MAI.

Quebec Sovereignty

It is difficult to imagine how Quebec nationalists would buy into a more decentralized and market-driven model of Canadian federalism. Yet, the sovereigntist government of Lucien Bouchard has certainly bought into the big business agenda in reorganizing the

Quebec economy. It has gone out of its way to cultivate alliances with major corporations in Quebec, several of which are linked to the BCNI. By giving top priority to reducing the deficit through slashing social programs and public services, the Bouchard government has tried to send a signal to transnational corporations that Quebec is open for business.

What is even more difficult to imagine is how Quebec sovereigntists can truly aspire to becoming a nation-state in a world order that is increasingly dominated by transnational corporations through global investment regimes like the MAI. After all, Quebec nationalism has traditionally put more weight on collective, as distinct from individual, rights. The original motto of modern Quebec nationalism was *maîtres chez nous*, masters in our own house. The legacy of René Lévesque was to establish the economic foundations of Quebec independence by nationalizing the hydro-electric power industry, creating an industrial development bank, and developing unique institutions like the Caisse de dépôt et placement. Yet these and many other cardinal features of the Quebec sovereigntist movement stand in direct contradiction to the new global trade regime. Indeed, the proposed rules and disciplines of the MAI would virtually put a stranglehold on a Quebec sovereigntist government striving to build a new nation based on these nationalist values and principles.

Take, for example, Quebec's financial institutions. To develop and promote an indigenous economy, Quebec has established a unique network of financial institutions ranging from the Caisse de dépôt to the Mouvement Desjardins and the Quebec Federation of Labour's Solidarity Fund. Under the proposed MAI rules for financial services, the Mouvement Desjardins would be compelled to operate much more like a commercial bank than a credit union. The Solidarity Fund's policy of lending primarily to Quebec companies would likely be charged with violating the national treatment clause requiring that foreign-based and Quebec corporations be treated on an equal basis. Not only would the Mouvement Desjardins feel increasing pressure to compete with foreign-based banks, but it could also become much more vulnerable to foreign takeovers, especially if certain MAI disciplines for most favoured nation treatment of financial services were adopted and current trends towards the deregulation of banks and financial institutions continued.

An independent Quebec government would also be severely constrained in its use of subsidies and incentives to stimulate the development of its economy, culture, and society. The extensive use of government subsidies to support Quebec's dairy farm industry, for example, would have to be subjected to national treatment rules. So too would Quebec Hydro's practice (known as "cross-subsidization") of providing electricity at below market value to local businesses and institutions. As noted earlier (see chapter five), any government subsidies for Quebec's new child care program or cultural development, both of which involve non-profit centres and non-profit cultural institutions, would have to be made available to foreign-based enterprises and institutions that specialize in those fields, even if the enterprises were for-profit. Similarly, government incentives to stimulate the development of key industries in Quebec in an overall effort to build an indigenous economy would likely be severely restricted under the MAI.

The fundamental fact is that the MAI would make it extremely difficult for an independent Quebec to exercise its rights to political self-determination. After declaring independence, the Quebec National Assembly would soon discover that, under the new global investment regime, it had been stripped of many of the tools and powers it needed to build its economy, culture, and society. Similar problems would likely arise if Quebec decided to remain in Canada and continue to build a "distinct" or "unique" society. Futhermore, the MAI could be used by Canada as well as other nation-states and transnational corporations to throw monkey wrenches into the plans of a pro-sovereigntist Quebec government. For example, with the Cree peoples and the Quebec government both claiming ownership and jurisdiction over a rich reservoir of natural resources in northern Quebec, and natural resources codified as an investment under the proposed treaty, it is conceivable that the MAI could be used as a tool by foreign states or corporations to intensify the dispute.

Provincial Powers

Normally, international trade agreements are binding on national governments alone. At most, only diplomatic remedies can be taken to influence the practices of subnational governments like our provinces. In the case of the WTO, for example, if an existing provincial law or program violates the agreement, the most that can be done is to pressure Ottawa by reinstating certain tariffs on Canadian exports. But a major objective of the MAI is to provide both member nation-states and transnational corporations with the tools they need to tackle subnational governments. By possessing the rights and powers to sue, foreign investors as well as states would be able to use binding international arbitration and domestic courts to enforce remedies against provincial laws and programs. This dramatic expansion of the pool of potential litigants would expose citizens to enormous liability arising from the new investment laws.

Although the final wording remains to be settled by the

negotiators, the inclusion of subnational governments in the application of the MAI rules and disciplines has serious implications for the reshaping of Canadian federalism. Under these conditions, devolving powers to the provinces could, in effect, render the provinces even more powerless. What good would it do, for example, to give the provinces responsibility for fisheries and forestry if it turns out that they are hampered by foreign corporations in issuing business licences based on residency or citizenship, or in reaping economic benefits through increased local processing, or in imposing controls on overfishing practices or clear-cut logging? What does it mean for the provinces to assume full control of agriculture and energy in this country if these same provinces have to abandon existing laws that limit or prohibit the ownership of farm lands by non-resident foreign citizens and restrict foreign ownership of water and electrical utilities?

In effect, a more decentralized federation could well become an empty shell. Sooner or later, provincial governments would discover that everyday practices they take for granted could be ruled out of order by the MAI. Government procurement practices designed to support local businesses by purchasing their goods and services may be prohibited. Government subsidies and incentives to strengthen local industries, to stimulate job creation for community residents, and even to promote the use of pollution control measures, could be severely restricted. Indeed, the ability of provincial governments to utilize conventional economic policy tools for broader public policy objectives would be considerably hindered under the MAI rules. Unless these policy tools are used in such a way as to favour foreign corporations and investors, they would be constantly vulnerable to challenge under the MAI.

The same problems would be faced by municipal governments. As creatures of the provinces, municipal governments would also be subject to the MAI rules, unless the negotiators agree otherwise before the treaty is ratified. With all the downloading that is taking place these days, municipal governments could find themselves severely constrained when it comes to contracting out services. If, for example, municipal governments decided to save revenues by contracting out their fire protection and waste disposal services, they would be obligated to open up the bidding to foreign firms. When it comes to purchasing goods and services, municipal governments would be under the same performance restrictions as their federal and provincial cousins. And given the fact that many municipal governments are involved in providing subsidies to non-profit community groups for education, health, social, and cultural services, they would likely be compelled to make these subsidies equally available to foreign-based agencies.

Beyond that, provincial governments would find themselves drawn into a highly competitive form of federalism under the MAI. Without any national obligations and standards for social programs and public services, both foreign-based and domestic corporations would be in a position to play provinces against one another. The end result is competitive poverty and a race to the bottom. It could be argued that this kind of competitive federalism already exists under the AIT. The big difference, however, is that unlike the AIT, the MAI would have binding enforcement mechanisms. Moreover, the MAI would provide these mechanisms to transnational corporations as well as national governments.

Aboriginal Self-Government

The political rights of Canada's First Nations are also in danger of being eclipsed by the new trade and investment regimes. When the Constitution was repatriated in 1982, the government entrenched the basic rights of aboriginal peoples and the fiduciary responsibilities of Ottawa that had been embodied in pre-Confederation documents (like the Royal Proclamation of 1783) and modern-day treaties. It is on the basis of these historical documents that the First Nations today have reasserted their rights to self-government. In early 1997, the Royal Commission Report on Aboriginal Peoples strongly reaffirmed these historic rights.

Since the infamous 1969 White Paper, Ottawa has been gradually moving to the point where it could off-load to the provinces its fiduciary responsibilities for aboriginal peoples. Initially, federal spending powers were used to entice provincial governments to provide programs and services to aboriginal peoples. The Mulroney government declared that "off reserve" Indians would be the responsibility of the provinces. In turn, the Chrétien government began to take steps to dismantle the Department of Indian and Northern Affairs and to devolve powers and responsibilities to local band councils. Indian Affairs minister Ron Irwin introduced the so-called "inherent rights" policy, which, among other things, not only required provincial governments to be involved but gave them a veto in negotiations on devolution. Through its Financial Transfers agreements, Ottawa also compelled First Nations to submit to provincial laws in the delivery of programs and services. While these measures ostensibly were meant to bring about greater aboriginal self-government, they created what amounted to a modified version of municipal government.

In 1996, Irwin proposed sixty-three amendments to the Indian Act based on a very limited consultation with aboriginal communities. The amendments were sharply rejected by Ovide Mercredi, then the national chief of the Assembly of First Nations (AFN), as being an attempt to assist banks, trust companies, and big business. They were designed to address issues "that are not coming from our people," said Mercredi. "The whole drafting that has been done behind the scenes by bureaucrats is geared to satisfy the business community that wants to do business with Indian people." Acknowledging that there are aboriginals who "want to use the property of their people for their own economic interest," Mercredi charged that the proposed amendments to the Indian Act would open the door for aboriginal peoples "to lose their land in business deals." Whether by design or default, the amendments would be largely compatible with the emerging MAI rules.

In the spiritual traditions of most First Nations, the land is understood to be Mother Earth, which, in turn, belongs to the Great Spirit. As a result, land is collectively owned and shared by all members of the community, and the notion of private property is seen as an alien concept. Yet, according to an AFN-commissioned legal analysis of the proposed Indian Act amendments, several of the changes would insert a legal definition of land based on the notion of individual property rights. Other amendments proposed that band councils be established or designated as corporations. The implication is that the Chief and Council would constitute the board of directors of a corporation, which, in turn, would be recognized as the holder of reserve land. In effect, reserve lands would become corporate property rather than communal lands owned by all members of the First Nation community.

Although the Indian Act amendments were supposed to reduce federal powers and responsibilities over aboriginal communities, they would strengthen Ottawa's role when it comes to exercising control over certain kinds of resource developments. In terms of forestry, for example, the powers of the federal cabinet "to make regulations about the cutting, removal and disposition of timber" would be increased. The authority of the Indian Affairs minister to grant licences for these activities would also be expanded, thereby imposing further limits on the capacities of First Nations to exercise self-government. Furthermore, the amendments would augment the "power of cabinet to make law about mines and minerals exploration, development, production, processing and removal." In other words, the proposal suggests that Ottawa has no intention of handing control over strategic resources like minerals and timber to First Nations, especially given the federal government's commitments under NAFTA and the obligations it would face under the MAI.

For the time being, the legislation to amend the Indian Act has been withdrawn by the new minister, Jane Stewart, in response to strong opposition from First Nations communities. Even so, the proposed legislation indicates how far the Chrétien government might be prepared to go. And whether or not the Indian Act amendments are passed, the MAI rules are to be applied to all subnational governments, including those of First Nations. In other words, First Nations would be subjected to the same restrictions as any other level of government in providing for the economic, social, cultural, environmental, and political rights of their peoples.

Constitutional Quagmire

Meanwhile, the political rights and powers accorded to transnational corporations (as well as the OECD member states) under the MAI raise some serious legal and constitutional problems, not the least of which is the foreign investors' ability to use domestic courts to seek damages or legal rulings in their favour. "While international arbitration panels might be friendlier for foreign investors," says a study prepared for the Western Governors Association in the U.S., "access to domestic courts gives them the ability to seek injunctions to stop enforcement of offending laws, a power that international arbitrators do not have." The question of how the panels or courts would function to resolve disputes raised in Canada, let alone twenty-eight other nation-states, is a complicated one.

If the U.S. Congress adopts the MAI, it has the constitutional authority to make it binding on all the states through its implementing legislation. Canada does not have a similar power to make the MAI binding on the provinces; in fact, any attempt to do so could provoke a constitutional battle if the provinces decide to challenge Ottawa's authority. Further, it is not at all clear whether foreign investors with a grievance against a provincial government would be able to bring direct legal claims against the province or whether they would have to sue Ottawa first. And if provincial laws are contested before an international arbitration forum, who would defend them, Ottawa or the provincial government?

When charges are brought by OECD member states or their transnational corporations against Canada or the provinces, the MAI rules would have supremacy over Canadian laws, federal or provincial. Canadian laws would only be relevant when consistent with the MAI rules. Moreover, when foreign states and corporations take their claims before international arbitration panels, those panels are not bound to follow established Canadian law in these matters. On the contrary, U.S. constitutional laws such as the takings rule are likely to prevail. Even if cases are brought before Canadian courts, as we noted earlier, the Charter of Rights and Freedoms can be used to support basic elements of the U.S. takings law. As a result, judgments are likely to award foreign investors both property rights and legal remedies that go far beyond those that domestic investors are granted in Canadian courts. While it may be possible for Canadian corporations, through joint ventures or their subsidiaries, to bring claims under the MAI rules and procedures, serious questions could arise as to whether domestic investors could any longer be guaranteed equal protection before the law.

All this leads to the question of how damages are to be awarded and recouped. The issue becomes more complicated if a provincial government and its laws are the target of a foreign investor's claim. Once again, a lot depends on who is named as the principal party — Ottawa or the provincial government whose laws are in dispute. If Ottawa is the named party, then how would damages be recouped? Would Ottawa be able to withhold federal funds in order to pay the damages? Or would the federal government have to sue the "offending" provincial government in order to recoup the monetary damages? These are only a few of the sticky legal wranglings that are likely to emerge under the MAI.

Citizen Disenfranchisement

Even if all of these many legal and constitutional issues were satisfactorily resolved, the fundamental problem with the MAI would remain: the denigration of citizens and their political rights in a democratic society. In the new world order, where the WTO and the MAI not only establish trade and investment rules but also function like global constitutions, it is transnational corporations that have real citizenship status and political rights. Wherever they go — Citizen Exxon or Citizen Ford, Citizen Mitsubishi or Citizen Shell, Citizen Sony or Citizen GE, Citizen IBM or Citizen Microsoft, Citizen Pepsi or Citizen McDonald's — their political rights as investors are constitutionally guaranteed and protected.

The irony is that corporations are fast being granted first-class citizenship rights at a time when people in Canada and elsewhere in the world are losing whatever basic democratic rights they have managed to achieve through prolonged struggle. Of course, this is what we have been trying to chronicle throughout these pages. In our view, the systematic dismantling of the economic, social, cultural, and environmental rights that were enshrined fifty years ago in the Universal Declaration will be accelerated and consolidated if a global investment regime like the MAI is ratified. And who will answer for the outcome? Institutions like NAFTA, the WTO, and the proposed MAI are not only designed but operated by a clique of government and corporate bureaucrats with little or no public accountability. Citizen movements are systematically excluded from the decision-making process. Unless people, not only here in Canada but throughout the world, can effectively participate in decisions affecting their lives, there is little or no chance that they will gain control over their economic, social, cultural, and environmental futures.

In short, the great tragedy that underlies the MAI as an instance of global constitution-making is that it contributes to a deeply undemocratic world order, one made up of two classes of citizens: faceless corporate super-citizens with virtually unfettered economic power, and whole populations of politically disenfranchised people with their rights stripped away.

EIGHT

WE CAN
SAY NO

During the 1980s and early 1990s, Canadians from all walks of life became involved in the fight against the FTA and NAFTA. Although the majority of Canadians knew these deals were bad for their country, global and domestic business pressure persuaded governments to adopt them. Most of us were left exhausted by the fight and discouraged by the loss. We were forced to redirect our remaining energies to resisting cutbacks on the home front and dealing with the aftermath of the new treaties. It is time to turn our minds back to the global arena and get involved again.

As the preceding chapters have shown, the MAI dangerously places Canada at the mercy of stateless capital. Statistics Canada reports that in 1996 our country was the third-largest recipient of foreign direct investment in the world — about $15 billion that year. The *total* value of FDI in Canada is now about $180 billion, making our per capita level of investment roughly six times that of the U.S. According to the Canadian Centre for Policy Alternatives, U.S. investors alone increased their ownership of Canadian bonds by 228 percent between 1988 and 1995. This disproportionately high level of foreign investment would leave Canada particularly vulnerable to MAI challenges by the foreign owners of these investments.

In recent years, it has become fashionable not to track whether investment is domestic or foreign. While the federal government used to monitor and publish the numbers quite closely, it is now more difficult to find statistics on foreign investment by sector. The agency that monitored foreign investment in energy has been shut down, and this function has not been picked up by another. Investment Canada, which replaced the old Foreign Investment Review Agency and which the government claims is still functioning, is not even listed in the federal government directory.

But the threat of the MAI forces us to reopen the books and see exactly who is in control. As transnational corporations become increasingly stateless, they operate outside of any national jurisdiction, and the global jurisdiction operates almost exclusively in their interest. In an MAI world, it would become even more urgent for companies to extricate themselves from the national interests of their countries of origin in order to compete with corporations that already have.

Canadians can ask, then, how it is that the federal government could put our interests at such risk by promoting the MAI. And make no mistake — Canada has been an MAI champion from the beginning. As early as November 1995, when the MAI was still intended to be endorsed by the WTO and not the OECD, then trade minister Art Eggleton hosted a meeting to bring undecided countries onside.

The explanation for the government's eagerness lies in another set of investment statistics, this time on Canadian investors abroad. At the same time that foreign money has been flowing into Canada, Canadian money has been flowing out. Canadian FDI total outflow is $170 billion. It is this sector and its interests that have influenced the Chrétien government to pursue the MAI; it would seem that Canadians with money — individual investors and Canadian corporations — are, to the feds, the most important Canadians of all.

New Brunswick MP Harold Culbert explains his government's support for the MAI in a letter to a constituent: "The government is working to see that Canadian firms like Corel, Northern Telecom, and Seagram have the same opportunities abroad that foreign companies enjoy here. Under NAFTA, Canada has already agreed on extensive investment rights and obligations with the United States and Mexico . . . The main objective is to extend these NAFTA rules to all OECD countries and to any country willing and able to join the MAI . . . The MAI would include rules governing the conditions for expropriation, prompt and effective compensation, and the unrestricted transfer of funds."

Culbert admits that the agreement "will limit the power of the government to discourage foreign investment" but adds, "it will, however, improve the situation of Canadian companies abroad."

In the following excerpt from its web site, the Department of Foreign Affairs and International Trade, responsible for the MAI, shows that it is clear about whom the MAI serves:

Canada would benefit from a comprehensive MAI in three ways:

1) by affording greater protection to Canadian direct investment in OECD and other MAI-adhering countries;

2) by advancing Canadian trade and investment interests abroad to the extent that the MAI reduces barriers or discrimination adversely affecting outward Canadian investment; and

3) by raising the attractiveness of Canada as an investment location through the undertaking of state-of-the-art obligations. The MAI could also serve as a model for an eventual WTO-based investment agreement.

No mention of social programs, Canadian culture, labour standards, or environmental rights. Canadians are reduced to the status of investors and consumers. Says journalist Janice Harvey, who quoted Harold Culbert's letter in her column for the Saint John *Telegraph Journal*, "We have been slow to admit the Canadian government has willingly subjugated its power to govern to corporate interests but we can deny it no longer. Here it is, in our collective face."

The Chrétien government will undoubtedly deny the dangers outlined in these pages and call us fearmongers. They will probably claim that the MAI just extends the scope of NAFTA, which they now endorse after fighting free trade in the 1980s, and that we should trust them and not worry about such esoteric matters.

They will say that they are seeking protection for many of the concerns listed here; and indeed, Canada is seeking forty-eight country-specific reservations, considerably more than any other OECD country. They will claim that this shows their sensitivity to the concerns of social, cultural, and environmental groups and they will use the proposed reservations as proof that the MAI will not damage Canadian interests.

But as we've seen, any negotiated country-specific reservations will become a hit list. The roll-back clause is clearly intended to undo reservations one at a time; the best Canada could do would be to buy a little time for certain programs and policies. In any case, there is little chance that Canada will actually get the reservations on its wish list. The OECD Secretariat reported in November 1996 that "MAI negotiators are determined to keep [general exceptions and country-specific reservations] to a minimum." Negotiators close to the process say that most issues have been sorted out; it is the wording, not the purpose, that is still being debated.

Further, Canada is claiming these country-specific reservations on the national treatment provisions, but not on performance requirements, dispute settlement, or other clauses; the government may still be vulnerable in these areas, even if it negotiates several exemptions. Lawyers for Ethyl Corporation, in bringing their case dealing with MMT to a Senate committee, have based their arguments on just these unprotected clauses.

Nor should Canadians be consoled by the promise of wording to protect the environment and labour standards in the preamble to the MAI. Such provisions would be entirely voluntary and constitute no binding commitment on the parties whatsoever. In fact, raising these issues in the preamble could give the false impression that these areas are protected in the MAI when in fact they are not.

For a true picture of Canada's intentions on the environment and labour, we look to the confidential minutes of a July 2, 1997, meeting of the MAI Negotiating Group (NG), at which standards were discussed. "The remainder of the discussion focused mainly on the nature and the elements to be included in the provision on not lowering [environmental and labour] standards. A growing number of countries [were] in favour of making such a provision binding," said the minutes, which went on to list these countries. Canada was not one of them.

Reporter Mark Abley of the Montreal *Gazette* writes about Canada's record on the environment at the WTO:

> A thriving commerce exists, largely from rich states to poor, in materials that are prohibited domestically as dangerous to life or health: toxic chemicals and insecticides, for instance. Many nations want such trade to be regulated, even banned. Not Canada. Our government argued that responsibility ought to rest with the importer. In other words, nations should be free to export abroad what they ban at home.
>
> Or take the question of sustainability. Many pressure groups, and a few countries, encourage "eco-labelling" — a practice that informs consumers whether a particular item was grown in a sustainable way. If a table is made of wood from a sustainable logged forest, an eco-label can trumpet the good news. Innocuous? Not to Canada. This country has asked the WTO to create formal rules on the subject — rules that might lead to the banning of some eco-labels as camouflaged protectionism . . . The pressure on Ottawa is believed to have come from Canada's pulp-and-paper industry, notably the giant MacMillan Bloedel Ltd.

This demonstrates how hard we can expect the government to fight for our culture, social programs, and environmental protection as the MAI talks get down to the wire. As Canadians we must take it upon ourselves to apply counterpressure against the powerful influence of corporations. To do so, we suggest three steps. The first is to reclaim our rights as citizens.

A Citizens' Charter

In Canada, it has generally been recognized that all citizens have the fundamental rights found in the UN Declaration of 1948, including the right to effectively participate in decisions affecting them. Individuals secure these rights through the community — locally, nationally, and internationally. In our parliamentary system of democracy, the state has a moral and political obligation not only to carry out its electoral mandate, but to ensure these rights are realized through government policies and programs.

While the federal government seems to have abandoned its obligation to safeguard the solemn commitments it undertook fifty years ago, bowing to the pressure of the MAI and the other instruments of the global economy, our democratic rights as citizens are as valid as ever. Canadians can remind governments of their responsibilities by demanding that they:

1) reestablish and maintain universal, public social and educational services and standards for all citizens, including pensions, health care, family and social assistance, unemployment insurance, and child care;

2) reestablish and maintain cultural protections and programs for artists, writers, filmmakers, and musi-

cians, in order to promote the cultural heritage and diversity of the country and its citizens;

3) protect the natural resource, species, energy, and environmental heritage of the nation and establish laws to enforce this protection for its citizens and future generations of the nation;

4) protect and promote domestic farmers, food producers, and food systems to ensure the continuation of the family farm, a fair price at the farm gate, and food at a fair price for all citizens;

5) establish a fair taxation regime so that business, domestic and foreign, is subject to the same responsibilities as citizens to contribute to the well-being of the whole society;

6) develop a fair trade policy that preserves the capacity to meet national priorities for food, energy, technology, and other vital national resources and limit trade where necessary;

7) reestablish working standards, minimum wages, positive collective bargaining legislation, health and safety protection for workers, and a full-employment policy;

8) restrict the right of financial interests and lobbies to use their wealth to influence politicians or elections;

9) fulfil human rights obligations that outlaw discrimination based on age, sex, racial or ethnic background, and sexual orientation; and

10) enact law to ensure freedom of the press, restrict corporate concentration in the media, and maintain domestic control of press and broadcasting services.

Embracing a Citizens' Charter that includes all of these objectives would allow Canadians to declare our democratic and sovereign rights in a global economy; assert these rights in a more direct and personal manner; develop our own negotiating positions in facing governments and corporations; counter the dominant ideology of the new economy; build the kind of extra-parliamentary vehicles we need to reclaim these rights; and develop a progressive alternative vision for Canada as a sovereign and democratic nation-state.

Embracing a Citizens' Charter would also give us the courage to defy the cry of inevitability that so often stops us dead in our tracks. A global economy built in the image of stateless capital is not inevitable; it is a system created by those who have a great deal to gain from it. Knowing that we have the right to reject the MAI is a necessary first step to reclaiming our full heritage and reversing the culture of defeatism.

Citizens' Sovereignty

The second step in resisting the MAI is to propose another model for regulating transnational investment.

Saying "no" to the MAI does not mean that there should be no global investment treaty. Obviously, the rate of foreign direct investment is accelerating rapidly, and there is a need for international rules to regulate this movement. But we should be concerned about who sets the rules.

The prime architects of the MAI have been government bureaucrats acting in the interest of their transnational corporate clients. Their main objective has been to ensure that governments provide a safe and secure climate for profitable transnational investment and competition. To this end, they elected to adopt the "takings" rule of U.S. property rights law — which insists that corporations be fully compensated for any form of expropriation by governments — as the legal framework for the MAI. But this is certainly not the only way to design an investment treaty. There are alternatives.

As we noted earlier, the UN Charter of Economic Rights and Duties of States provided quite a different framework for establishing a set of global investment rules. It was based on the assumption that nation-states, acting on behalf of all their citizens and the public at large, had the political sovereignty to regulate foreign investment. The charter granted member nations the authority to supervise the operations of transnational corporations in their territories by establishing performance requirements.

These performance requirements were to be based on the national development needs of the people of each country. While nation-states were also granted the powers to "nationalize, expropriate or transfer ownership of foreign property," the charter called for the payment of fair compensation for expropriation.

Although changes in the global economy over the past twenty years or so would require that modifications be made, the UN Charter on the Economic Rights and Duties of States contains many of the elements for a modern, alternative approach to global investment rules. Unfortunately, nation-states like Canada have never been able to fully exercise what sovereign powers they may have had to control the operations of transnational corporations in their domain. And in today's global economic climate, the difficulties involved in regulating foreign investment have become much more acute.

In opposing the MAI, therefore, it is imperative that a new model for establishing investment rules be put forward for public discussion and debate. This would involve defining a clear set of investment criteria to ensure that corporations, both domestic and foreign, contribute to the economic, social, cultural, and ecological goals of national development.

Based on these criteria, performance standards and requirements would be set on a range of priorities, including job content and appropriate technology; labour standards and pollution controls; domestic ownership and cultural content criteria; worker safety and food safety standards; and export quotas on natural resources. These kinds of performance requirements could be supplemented by other forms of legislation stipulating, for example, that corporations involved in plant closings meet certain conditions protective of workers and the community.

Measures would have to be taken to curb the mushrooming of corporate monopolies and speculative enterprises. One of the most effective ways for transnational corporations to subvert the political sovereignty of nation-states like Canada is by increasing concentration and ownership of key sectors of the economy through monopolies, mergers, and cartels. By reintroducing anti-trust legislation (which has been used before in other countries, including the U.S.), and vigorously applying it, it would be possible to break up corporate monopolies that are not acting in the public interest. (This would mean replacing the corporate-friendly Competition Act, drafted by the Business

Council on National Issues and passed by the Mulroney Conservatives in 1986.)

More than 90 percent of all foreign investment in Canada is used to acquire existing Canadian firms rather than establish new business enterprises. Not only do acquisitions like this mean no new jobs, they often lead to more layoffs as new owners streamline their operations. Legislation outlining performance requirements must be developed to control these kinds of speculative investments.

An alternative investment model could also include legislative action to repatriate the tens of billions of dollars in profits that both Canadian and foreign-based corporations move offshore every year to avoid paying their fair share of taxes and the costs of doing business in this country. While Canada abandoned the use of direct capital controls back in 1951, they are still used by some eleven industrialized and 109 developing countries to curb the flight of capital.

Just as police forces are now calling for the closer monitoring of global capital flow in order to restrict the laundering of drug money, so international agreements could be negotiated to require that capital crossing borders illegally is returned to the country of origin. This would require the negotiation of common international standards to determine what would be acceptable and unacceptable capital flow.

It would not be possible for Canada to pursue this course alone without incurring economic retaliation. To do so would be to embark on a suicide mission. But there are some member states of the OECD, notably several of the Nordic countries in Europe, and certainly many developing countries, who share our trepidation about the MAI. In these countries, there is still a relatively strong political tradition that holds that nation-states, acting in the interest of their citizens, have a moral obligation to regulate foreign investment and apply performance standards to the operations of corporations.

It could be argued that nation-states like Canada must exercise this kind of political sovereignty over foreign investment to ensure that the basic democratic rights and needs of their citizens are met. This, in turn, is essential for public order and national security. Keith Kelly of the CCA proposes that Canadians define our national security rights in terms of the protection of our environmental, social, and cultural heritage. "Perhaps now is the time for Canada to redefine 'national security' by including those areas and values, such as cultural sovereignty, which we consider integral to the maintenance of the Canadian state." In other words, citizen security must supersede corporate security if we are to see the continuance of Canada as a distinct nation-state.

Citizens' Resistance

The third step is action-oriented — building the political resistance needed to defeat the MAI at the OECD meeting in May 1998, or, failing that, to prevent the Canadian government from implementing the new treaty.

Although the Canadian government does not need parliamentary approval for an international agreement (unlike the U.S., which must go to Congress for ratification), Parliament does have to give its consent to any legislative changes required by the agreement. Only after this "implementing legislation" is given passage can Canada deposit an "instrument of ratification" with the OECD, indicating the country's readiness to comply with the obligations of the MAI. Thus, Canadians will have a chance to influence this process directly.

In generating opposition to the MAI, it is important for citizens to take a proactive, offensive stance. This is precisely what a Citizens' Charter coupled with a reassertion of Citizens' Sovereignty can do. The task of building popular resistance to the OECD plans, however, must begin with those constituencies that are going to be directly and dramatically affected by the proposed MAI regime. These constituencies include women, unemployed workers, senior citizens, low-income Canadians, educators, health care and child care workers, public servants, artists, filmmakers, writers, book publishers, farmers, small businesses, First Nations peoples, and all those who work in social, environmental, cultural, or labour advocacy and in international development.

For all of these sectors, the challenge is to make building resistance to the MAI a strategic priority. The MAI is not just another issue to be added to an already overloaded agenda. Instead, it can be seen as a kind of theme that permeates all other policy issues. To be sure, building a campaign of resistance will require energy and resources. But once a sense of urgency is established, opposition can be mounted on several fronts.

COMMUNITY FRONT: The local community could well emerge as an important vanguard in the battle against the MAI. Unlike the FTA and NAFTA, the MAI will directly affect municipal governments, by seriously hindering their ability to implement their own local policies and programs. In their relationship with provincial governments, municipal councils are directly involved in delivering services that will be affected by the MAI, such as public education, social housing, health care, and social assistance. Many municipal governments have their own procurement programs for purchasing goods and services to help local economies and job creation.

The MAI could also affect municipal regulations on local real estate, bank loans for and investment in community development, and the privatization of public services ranging from garbage collection to libraries. Community forums must be organized in the months ahead to stimulate local awareness, discussion, and debate. Campaigns could also be mounted to have municipal councils declare their jurisdictions MAI-free zones.

PROVINCIAL FRONT: Provincial governments could become deal-breakers. As noted earlier, Ottawa cannot legally bind the provinces to a deal like the MAI in the same way that Washington can bind all fifty-one states in the U.S. Research is needed to show how provincial laws, policies, and programs could be adversely affected by the MAI, with specific attention given to the use of government procurement programs, subsidies, and incentives. Impacts on public education, crown agencies, health care delivery, and the privatization of various public services should be studied. Environmental regulations affecting forestry, mining, and energy developments should also be examined along with foreign ownership restrictions on agricultural lands and real estate.

At the same time, there are major corporate players on the provincial economic scene that stand to gain from the new investment rules; they must be identified and profiled. Provincial governments should be pressured to hold public hearings on the MAI. In some provinces, it might even be possible to pass a motion declaring opposition to, and non-compliance with, the proposed MAI rules and disciplines.

NATIONAL FRONT: In mounting its own campaign to sell the MAI, Ottawa will likely try to emphasize that it does not differ substantially from NAFTA and that Canada's interests will be protected by reservations and exemptions. A counter-campaign should highlight the new and expanded powers given to transnational corporations under the MAI and the fact that any reservation granted for non-conforming law, policies, or programs will only be temporary.

This campaign must also emphasize how Ottawa's hands will be tied when it comes to job creation, cultural sovereignty, social programs (especially public health care and public pensions), environmental safeguards, and real constitutional reforms. A nonpartisan pressure group, composed of MPs from several parties, could bring the issue to the new session of Parliament, where the Chrétien government could be urged to hold debates, conduct all-party cross-country hearings, and strike parliamentary committees to study the impacts of the MAI on various policy areas.

Concerned groups should concentrate on unmasking and challenging the vested interests at stake for Canadian-based transnational corporations. Who are the natural resource giants working to tear apart our environmental regulations? Who are the private health and pension companies that would prosper from the privatization of these sectors? Who are the corporate players keen to dismantle Canadian content rules in culture? If we don't know who these companies and their executives are and if we don't understand the power they exert behind the scenes, we will make the mistake of focusing only on politicians, who have lost or given away a great deal of clout in the global economy.

INTERNATIONAL FRONT: The only way to effectively block a global treaty like the MAI is to build an international movement of political opposition. In many countries, citizen movements are in the process of organizing campaigns. The Third World Network, an alliance of more than 600 public advocacy groups headquartered in Malaysia, helped halt the MAI lobby at the Singapore meeting of the WTO. Public Citizen has picked up the fight in the U.S., along with the majority of U.S. environmental groups. The labour movement in France has committed itself to defeating the MAI. Groups in New Zealand and Australia have put the MAI directly in the spotlight.

Labour unions and social organizations, in Canada and these other regions, must band together to share information and assist the development of campaigns in their respective countries. Part of their strategy should involve identifying contradictory positions taken and statements made by governments trying to sell the MAI to their citizens.

During the months leading up to the OECD ministerial meetings in May 1998, this kind of solidarity networking can be very useful in mobilizing widespread opposition to the MAI. Canadian, European, and American activists are now working with key social and political movements in Third World countries to understand the new imperialism embodied in the MAI and to prepare for the expected attempts to use the accession clause to rope in countries from the South.

The time has come to stop the MAI. Its passage would signify the global conquest of the Washington Consensus over the UN Declaration and all that it represents. And because it locks in the signatories for twenty years, it would bind another generation to the values and ideologies it embodies. It was one thing for capitalism to have taken on communism; but, if the MAI is ratified, the new target will be democracy itself. We cannot allow this assault to succeed.

We can say no.

CRITICAL EXCERPTS FROM THE LATEST MAI TEXT

The following are several key clauses from the May 1997 draft text of the MAI, the most recent edition available at time of printing. As negotiations are still under way, this draft may differ from the text that is eventually settled upon. Nevertheless, the following excerpts demonstrate the intent of the drafters and much, if not all, of what is contained here will likely form the heart of the final text of the MAI. The excerpts below are preceded by our own brief explanations (in italics).* Square brackets indicate areas still under negotiation.

National Treatment and Most Favoured Nation Treatment
"National treatment" requires countries to treat foreign investors and investments no less favourably than domestic ones. Countries could not, given this provision, place special restrictions on what foreign investors can own, maintain economic assistance programs that solely benefit domestic companies, or require that a corporation hire a certain percentage of managers locally. Laws that have a discriminatory effect on foreign investors would be prohibited whether or not such discrimination is intentional. However, there would be nothing to stop governments from treating foreign corporations more favourably than domestic ones.

---

* Some of the explanations borrow from the work of the Preamble Center for Public Policy in Washington, D.C.

The "most favoured nation" provision requires governments to treat all foreign countries and all foreign investors equally with respect to regulatory laws. Laws preventing corporations from doing business in countries with poor human rights practices would likely be prohibited by this clause.

1. Each Contracting Party shall accord to investors of another Contracting Party and to their investments, treatment no less favourable than the treatment it accords [in like circumstances] to its own investors and their investments with respect to the establishment, acquisition, expansion, operation, management, maintenance, use, enjoyment and sale or other disposition of investments.

2. Each Contracting Party shall accord to investors of another Contracting Party and to their investments, treatment no less favourable than the treatment it accords [in like circumstances] to investors of any other Contracting Party or of a non-Contracting Party, and to the investments of investors of any other Contracting Party or of a non-Contracting Party, with respect to the establishment, acquisition, expansion, operation, management, maintenance, use, enjoyment, and sale or other disposition of investments.

3. Each Contracting Party shall accord to investors of another Contracting Party and to their investments the better of the treatment required by Articles 1.1 and 1.2, whichever is the more favourable to those investors or investments.

Performance Requirements

These clauses place limits on laws that require investors to meet certain conditions before they may establish an enterprise in a particular locale or if they wish to be eligible for tax incentives or other government aid. Rules requiring corporations to use domestic inputs, set local content, hire Canadians, transfer technology, meet certain research and development commitments, or balance exports and imports could all be affected.

1. A Contracting Party shall not, in connection with the establishment, acquisition, expansion, management, operation or

conduct of an investment in its territory of an investor of a Contracting Party or of a non-Contracting Party, impose, enforce or maintain any of the following requirements, or enforce any commitment or undertaking:

a) to export a given level or percentage of goods or services;

b) to achieve a given level or percentage of domestic content;

c) to purchase, use or accord a preference to goods produced or services provided in its territory, or to purchase goods or services from persons in its territory;

d) to relate in any way the volume or value of imports to the volume or value of exports or to the amount of foreign exchange inflows associated with such investment;

e) to restrict sales of goods or services in its territory that such investment produces or provides by relating such sales to the volume or value of its exports or foreign exchange earnings;

f) to transfer technology, a production process or other proprietary knowledge to a natural or legal person in its territory, except when the requirement is imposed or the commitment or undertaking is enforced by a court, administrative tribunal or competition authority to remedy an alleged violation of competition laws [or to act in a manner not inconsistent with articles . . . of the TRIPS Agreement];

g) to locate its headquarters for a specific region or the world market in the territory of that Contracting Party;

h) to supply one or more of the goods that it produces or the services that it provides to a specific region or the world market exclusively from the territory of that Contracting Party;

[i) to achieve a given level or value of production, investment, sales, employment, or research and development in its territory;]

[j) to hire a given level of [local personnel] [nationals];]

k) to establish a joint venture; or

[l) to achieve a minimum level of local equity participation.]

Standstill and the Listing of Country-Specific Reservations

"Standstill" requires national and subnational governments to refrain from passing any future law that violates MAI rules. Standstill freezes the principles of national treatment and most favoured nation at their current level. Countries agree to list all their existing non-conforming measures, to impose no new ones, and to make no amendments to existing measures that would increase non-conformity to the MAI.

1. The MAI aims to ensure a high minimum standard of treatment for investors and their investments, including National Treatment and MFN treatment. Standstill would result from the prohibition of new or more restrictive exceptions to this minimum standard of treatment. From this perspective, a violation of standstill would be a violation of the underlying MAI obligations (e.g. of National Treatment and MFN), and the dispute settlement provisions would apply to such breaches of the MAI obligations.

2. Standstill would not apply, however, to any general exceptions (e.g. national security) or to any temporary derogations (e.g. balance of payments) that might be allowed under the MAI.

3. For those matters where Contracting Parties are ready to commit to standstill, the Drafting Group considered that:
   a) each Contracting Party should list all non-conforming measures in an Annex of the Agreement;
   b) the reservations should describe, in the most precise terms possible, the nature and scope of the non-conforming measures. This would ensure that the scope of the reservations is not broader than these measures and, thus, that the reservations are not of a "precautionary" nature;
   c) no additional non-conforming measures could be introduced; and
   d) an amendment to a non-conforming measure would be permitted provided it did not decrease the conformity of the measure.

Rollback

This provision requires national and subnational governments to eliminate laws, either immediately or over a period of time, that violate MAI rules. Countries agree to reduce and eventually eliminate non-conforming measures, including those listed as "country-specific reservations."

1. Rollback is the liberalisation process by which the reduction and eventual elimination of non-conforming measures to the MAI would take place. It is a dynamic element linked with standstill, which provides its starting point. Combined with standstill, it would produce a "ratchet effect", where any new liberalisation measures would be "locked in" so they could not be rescinded or nullified over time.

2. There are a number of ways for achieving rollback. The most commonly known in the trade field is that of successive rounds of negotiations where rollback results from the trade-offs or exchange of trade concessions. Peer pressure through periodic examinations of Member countries' restrictions has been the approach of the OECD liberalisation instruments. Rollback commitments may also be inscribed in schedules of commitments or list *[sic]* of reservations. While this has not been a generalised practice, it has been done in some cases under the OECD instruments.

3. Rollback might be achieved through:

    a) liberalisation commitments by the Contracting Parties effective on the date of entry into force of the MAI. This would imply that that *[sic]* not all restrictions currently maintained would be included in the list of reservations of the Contracting Parties;

    b) rollback commitments inscribed in a country reservation or description of a non-conforming measure by means of a "phase-out" or a "sunset clause" specifying a future date when the non-conforming measure would be removed or made more limited in the future. Phase-out or sunset provisions could not be envisaged for all non-conforming measures. They might be useful, however, where the phase-out of a non-conforming measure is inscribed in domestic legislation or where a Contracting Party is able to commit itself to future liberalisation by a specified date.

4. Rollback after the entry into force of the MAI could result from:

   a) an obligation for a Contracting Party to adjust its reservations to reflect any new liberalisation measure (the "ratchet" effect).

   b) periodic examinations of non-conforming measures. These examinations could lead to recommendations in favour of the removal or limitations of specific measures. These reviews could be conducted on a country-to-country basis, or on an horizontal or sectoral basis, taking into account the degree of liberalisation already achieved; and

   c) future rounds of negotiations designed to remove non-conforming measures. The decision to launch future negotiations could be taken at the conclusion of the MAI negotiations or the MAI could provide a specific date for the first round of such negotiations.

5. The "Parties Group" could have the role of monitoring the adjustment of country reservations, conducting periodic examinations of non-conforming measures or launching future rounds of negotiations.

Disputes Between an Investor and a Contracting Party

These provisions on investor-state dispute resolution enable private investors and corporations to sue national governments, and seek monetary compensation, in the event that a law, practice, or policy violates investor rights as established in the MAI. International investors would have the option to sue a country before an international tribunal rather than in the country's domestic courts. Essentially, investor-state dispute resolution confers on private investors the same rights and legal standing as national governments in enforcing the MAI's terms.

1. Scope and Standing

   a) This article applies to disputes between a Contracting Party and an investor of another Contracting Party concerning an alleged breach of an obligation of the former under this Agreement which causes loss or damage to the investor or its investment.

b) An investor of another Contracting Party may also submit to arbitration under this article any investment dispute concerning any obligation which the Contracting Party has entered into with regard to a specific investment of the investor through:

   i. an investment authorisation granted by its competent authorities specifically to the investor or investment;

   ii. a written agreement granting rights with respect to [categories of subject matters] on which the investor has relied in establishing, acquiring, or significantly expanding an investment.

2. Means of Settlement

Such a dispute should, if possible, be settled by negotiation or consultation. If it is not so settled, the investor may choose to submit it for resolution:

a) to any competent courts or administrative tribunals of the Contracting Party to the dispute;

b) in accordance with any dispute settlement procedure agreed upon prior to the dispute arising; or

c) by arbitration in accordance with this Article under *[any of a number of specified international arbitration panels]*.

. . .

14. Applicable law

a) Issues in dispute under paragraph 1(a) of this article shall be decided in accordance with this Agreement, interpreted and applied in accordance with the applicable rules of international law.

b) Issues in dispute under paragraph 1(b) of this article shall be decided in accordance with such rules of law as may be agreed by the parties to the dispute. In the absence of such agreement, such issues shall be decided in accordance with the law of the Contracting Party to the dispute (including its rules on the conflict of the laws), the law governing the authorisation or agreement and such rules of international law as may be applicable.

...

16. Final awards
    a) The arbitral tribunal, in its award, shall set out its findings of law and fact, together with the reasons therefor and may, at the request of a party, provide the following forms of relief:
       i. a declaration that the Contracting Party has failed to comply with its obligations under the this *[sic]* Agreement;
       ii. pecuniary compensation, which shall include interest from the time the loss or damage was incurred until time of payment;
       iii. restitution in kind in appropriate cases, provided that the Contracting Party may pay pecuniary compensation in lieu thereof where restitution is not practicable; and
       iv. with the Agreement of the parties to the dispute, any other form of relief.
    b) In appropriate cases where the loss or damage was incurred by an investment which remains a going concern, the tribunal may direct that the compensation or restitution be made to the investment.
    c) An arbitration award shall be final and binding between the parties to the dispute and shall be carried out without delay by the party against whom it is issued, subject to its post-award rights under the arbitral systems utilised.

Investment Protection

Clauses on expropriation and compensation ban the uncompensated expropriation of corporate assets. The definition of expropriation would include not just the outright seizure of property, but also government actions "tantamount to expropriation," which could include, for example, environmental regulations having a negative impact on the commercial interests of a foreign investor.

The MAI bans restrictions on the repatriation of profits and the movement of capital. Countries would not be able to prevent an investor from moving profits from the operation or sale of a local enterprise to that investor's home country. Nor could countries delay or prohibit transfers of assets, including financial instruments like stocks or currency.

1.1 Each Contracting Party shall accord to investments in its territory of investors of another Contracting Party fair and equitable treatment and full and constant protection and security. In no case shall a Contracting Party accord treatment less favourable than that required by international law.

1.2 A Contracting Party shall not impair by [unreasonable or discriminatory] [unreasonable and discriminatory] measures the operation, management, maintenance, use, enjoyment or disposal of investments in its territory of investors of another Contracting Party.

2.1 A Contracting Party shall not expropriate or nationalise directly or indirectly an investment in its territory of an investor of another Contracting Party or take any measure or measures having equivalent effect (hereinafter referred to as "expropriation") except:

a) for a purpose which is in the public interest;

b) on a non-discriminatory basis;

c) in accordance with due process of law; and

d) accompanied by payment of prompt, adequate and effective compensation in accordance with Articles 2.2 to 2.5 below.

2.2 Compensation shall be paid without delay.

2.3 Compensation shall be equivalent to the fair market value of the expropriated investment immediately before the expropriation occurred. The fair market value shall not reflect any change in value occurring because the expropriation had become publicly known earlier.

2.4 Compensation shall be fully realisable and freely transferable.

. . .

4.1 Each Contracting Party shall ensure that all payments relating to an investment in its territory of an investor of another Contracting Party may be freely transferred into and out of its territory without delay. Such transfers shall include, in particular, though not exclusively:

a) the initial capital and additional amounts to maintain or increase an investment;

b) returns;

c) payments made under a contract including a loan agreement;

d) proceeds from a sale or liquidation of all or any part of an investment;

e) payments of compensation under Articles 2 and 3;

f) payments arising out of the settlement of a dispute;

g) earnings and other remuneration of personnel engaged from abroad in connection with an investment.

. . .

[4.6 Notwithstanding Articles 4.1 to 4.5, a Contracting Party may prevent a transfer through the equitable, non-discriminatory and good faith application of measures to protect the rights of creditors, relating to or ensuring compliance with laws and regulations on the issuing, trading and dealing in securities, futures and derivatives, reports or records of transfers, or in connection with criminal offences and orders or judgements in administrative and adjudicatory proceedings, provided that such measures and their application shall not be used as a means of avoiding the Contracting Party's commitments or obligations under the Agreement.]

NOTES

CHAPTER ONE: The Rise and Fall of Democratic Rights

The United Nations Association in Canada was most helpful in research-ing and providing the key UN documents referred to in this chapter: the Universal Declaration of Human Rights and related Covenants, and the Charter of Economic Rights and Duties of States. We also used the excellent 1996 essay by Martin Khor of the Third World Network, *The WTO and the Proposed Multilateral Investment Agreement: Implications for Developing Countries and Proposed Solutions.* Elizabeth Smythe of Concordia University College of Alberta provided valuable historical con-text in her March 1997 paper, *Your Place or Mine? States, International Organizations and the Negotiation of Investment Rules: The OECD Versus the WTO,* as did David Schneiderman of the University of Alberta's Centre for Constitutional Studies in his paper of the same year, *Investment Rules and the New Constitutionalism: Inter-linkages and Disciplinary Effects.*

Two papers emerging from Public Citizen — Lori Wallach's *Background on the Multilateral Agreement on Investment Being Negotiated at the OECD* and Kristen Dawkins's *NAFTA, GATT and the World Trade Organization: The Emerging New World Order* — were excellent sources, as was the May 1997 briefing paper, *Writing the Constitution of a Single Global Economy: A Concise Guide to the Multilateral Agreement on Investment,* by Michelle Sforza-Roderick, Scott Nova, and Mark Weisbrot of the Washington-based Preamble Center for Public Policy.

We also used the declaration that came out of the WTO's December 1996 ministerial meeting in Singapore, various editions of *Inside U.S. Trade*, and several OECD documents pertaining to the MAI.

CHAPTER TWO: The Emergence of Global Corporate Rule

This chapter is a revised version of the preliminary analysis of the MAI prepared by Tony Clarke and published by the Canadian Centre for Policy Alternatives under the title *The Corporate Rule Treaty* in April 1997. We are indebted to Andrew Jackson of the Canadian Labour Congress and John Dillon of the Ecumenical Coalition for Economic Justice who provided notes identifying additional technical insights into specific MAI clauses and their connection with the FTA, NAFTA, and the GATT and the WTO. Two articles by David Schneiderman of the University of Alberta's Centre for Constitutional Studies contributed to our analysis: "NAFTA's Takings Rule: American Constitutionalism Comes to Canada," *University of Toronto Law Journal*, no. 46, 1996; and *Investment Rules and the New Constitutionalism: Interlinkages and Disciplinary Effects*, prepared for the Consortium on Globalization, Law and Social Science, New York University, April 1997. Also helpful for this chapter was Robert Stumberg of the Georgetown University Law Center in Washington, who assisted in the preparation of a paper on the MAI for the Western Governors Association. The Preamble Center for Public Policy briefing paper, *Writing the Constitution of a Single Global Economy*, also proved valuable.

The analysis of the proposed MAI rules and disciplines outlined in this chapter are based on a reading of two drafts of the text, dated January 13, 1997, and May 14, 1997; both were marked "confidential" and distributed by the OECD. While deliberate steps have been taken to avoid a heavy dose of technical legal jargon and extensive quotations from the text, the eight sets of "takings" discussed here are all related to specific clauses outlined in both draft texts. The few quotes in this chapter are taken directly from these draft texts. Use was made here of Schneiderman's analysis (cited above) of the "takings" rule. Reference to how the U.S. Supreme Court used the same Fourteenth Amendment to grant corporations the status of persons as it did to protect the rights of freed slaves was found in L. Rasmussen, *Earth Community Earth Ethics* (New York: Orbis Books, 1996). On the use of performance standards tied to subsidies and tax breaks, John Dillon points out that there has been an "evolution of stricter and stricter restrictions on performance standards" from the FTA through NAFTA (e.g., Article 1106:3) to the MAI, to the point that "each treaty is more confining than the last." It should be noted that the draft MAI texts reveal that the clause requiring public enterprises to "act solely in accordance with commercial considerations" was advanced by both Canada and the U.S. (using language adopted by NAFTA: see Article 1502:3 (b)).

CHAPTER THREE: The Assault on Economic Rights

For a short but useful summary of Canada's economic policy and rights tradition, see Maude Barlow and Bruce Campbell's *Straight Through the Heart* (Toronto: Harper Collins, 1995), chapter one and parts of chapters two and three. John Dillon's *Turning the Tide: Confronting the Money Traders*, published by the Canadian Centre for Policy Alternatives in 1996, contains insights on the role of the Bank of Canada in the development of economic policy. The challenge to the Chrétien government by the Business Council on National Issues was issued in a letter dated June 20, 1997, and co-signed by BCNI chair Al Flood and BCNI president and CEO Tom d'Aquino. For a summary of the dominant role played by the BCNI in directing Canadian economic policy over the past twenty years, see chapter one of Tony Clarke's *Silent Coup: Confronting the Big Business Takeover of Canada* (Ottawa: James Lorimer & Co. and Canadian Centre for Policy Alternatives, 1997). Analyses of the economic impacts of the MAI by both Andrew Jackson and Robert Stumberg were helpful for the development of this chapter. The potential impact of the MAI on the development of the Jobs and Timber Accord in British Columbia was discussed in *Monday* magazine, August 21, 1997. David Ranney's study of job creation under the free trade agreements (with Robert Naiman) is available from the Department of Urban Planning and Public Affairs at the University of Illinois in Chicago. Credit goes to Barbara Robson for identifying job creation programs in the Liberal Red Book II that might be challengeable under the MAI.

The story on the Nike takeover of Bauer was found in a *Globe and Mail* article by John Heinzl, July 2, 1997. For an insightful profile of Nike's Asian operations, see Cynthia Enloe's article, "The Globetrotting Sneaker," in *Ms* magazine, March–April 1997. For stats on the shifting patterns of foreign investment in Canada in an era of free trade, see John Dillon's

Turning the Tide. The minimum wage and poverty line figures from the National Council on Welfare were cited in a letter by Murray Dobbin to *The Globe and Mail,* July 15, 1997. The stats on the shocking disparities between CEO compensation packages and workers' wages were reported by the *CCPA Monitor,* vol. 3, no. 3, July–August, 1996. See also Appendix III of *Silent Coup.* The impact of the MAI on bank loans for community development and re-investment is discussed in the Preamble Center for Public Policy's briefing paper, *Writing the Constitution of a Single Global Economy.* The stats on women in low-paid employment were taken from a study published by the Canadian Labour Congress, *Women's Work: A Report* (June, 1997).

CHAPTER FOUR: The Threat to Environmental Rights

Steven Shrybman's superb spring 1997 analysis for the Common Front on the World Trade Organization, *An Environment Guide to the World Trade Organization,* was very helpful for this chapter, as was the Sierra Club's *Canada Five Years After Rio: Rio Report Card 1997.* The work and advice of Elizabeth May were invaluable. Barbara Robson's August 1997 research paper for Senator Mira Spivak, *Not a Done Deal: A Review of the Proposed Multilateral Agreement on Investment and Its Implications for National Sovereignty and Environmental Protection,* provided much insight. An April 1996 study by Leesteffy Jenkins, Robert Stumberg, Aileen Chang, and Lisa Irving for the Harrison Institute for Public Law at Georgetown University, *WTO Policy on Multilateral Environmental Agreements,* is an excellent reference, as is the series of briefing papers on the MAI distributed by Mark Vallianatos, with Friends of the Earth–U.S.

Public Citizen's *The WTO at 22 Months: Examples of Environmental and Health Threats,* prepared for a November 1996 meeting of the Canadian Common Front on the WTO, is chock full of information. Dave Bennett, national director of Health, Safety, and Environment for the Canadian Labour Congress, has written several excellent pieces, including *Beware ISO (International Organization for Standardization)* and *The WTO and the Environment: Six Policy Questions,* both of which were published in April 1997. The Philippine research institute, IBON, supplied the information on the 1995 Philippine Mining Act, and Alan Young of the Environmental Mining Council of British Columbia was most helpful in supplying data on Canadian mining companies abroad. Statistics Canada and Industry Canada were very helpful in the search for statistics on foreign ownership in the natural resource sector; one particularly useful source of figures in this area was *World Investment Report 1993: Transnational Corporations and Integrated International Production* (New York: United Nations Publications, 1993). Journalists Sean Fine, Laura Eggertson, and Anne McIlroy of *The Globe and Mail* and Ruth Abramson of *Maclean's* magazine were also good sources of information.

CHAPTER FIVE: The Demise of Social Rights

An overview of Canada's legacy of social programs is found in chapter one of Barlow and Campbell's *Straight Through the Heart.* For the distinctions to be made in the application of the MAI to Canada's mixed system of health care delivery, see Andrew Jackson's *A Note on the Multilateral Agreement on Investment (MAI) and Public and Social Services,* published by the Canadian Labour Congress in August 1997. Colleen Fuller's forthcoming book *Caring for Profits* (soon to be published by New Star Books) contains an analysis of the private, for-profit health care corporations that pose a threat to Canada's public health care system. See also Joyce Nelson's article, "Dr. Rockefeller Will See You Now," in *Canadian Forum,* January–February 1995, which identifies some of the hidden players at work in privatizing health care in Canada. A revealing profile of U.S. health care giant Columbia/HCA, entitled "A Hospital Chain's Brass Knuckles, and the Backlash," was published by the *New York Times,* May 11, 1997. For background information on the increasing role of big business in public education, see Maude Barlow and Heather-jane Robertson's *Class Warfare* (Toronto: Key Porter, 1994).

Insights on how big U.S. corporations plan to profit from growing involvement in social security reforms are described by Barbara Ehrenreich in her *Harper's* magazine article, "Spinning the Poor into Gold," August 1997. The connections between privatization and the potential corporate takeover of Canada's health, education, and social security systems are discussed in Tony Clarke's *Silent Coup,* especially chapters three, four, and five. John Dillon and Andrew Jackson provided further insights into the impact of the proposed MAI rules on Canada's system of public and social service delivery. On the issue of food security, the domination of Codex Alimentarius (which is responsible for setting global food standards) by transnational food corporations is outlined in *Codex Alimentarius Commission: Canada at the Codex*, prepared by Elisabeth Sterken, February 1997. The research department of the Canadian Union of Public Employees has been doing profiles on the emerging corporate players in health care and other public and social services, with references to the potential impacts of the MAI.

CHAPTER SIX: The War on Cultural Rights

Keith Kelly of the Canadian Conference of the Arts was most helpful in the preparation of this chapter. CCA documents that were also helpful include the September 1997 *Backgrounder on International Trade Agreements: GATT and the MAI*, the February 1997 *Backgrounder on Key Federal Measures Supporting the Production and Distribution of Canadian Cultural Products*, the November 1995 brief to the Standing Committee on Finance, *Building a Vision of a New Canada*, and regular editions of the CCA *Bulletin*. Culture analyst Paul Audley was another advisor, whose excellent forthcoming book for Stoddart, *Culture or Commerce? Canadian Culture After Free Trade*, will be a real addition to the debate in Canada. The University of Laval's Ivan Bernier shared his solid analysis in a June 1997 paper for the Centre for Trade Policy and Law, *Cultural Goods and Services in International Trade Law*.

The *1997 Alternative Federal Budget* put out by the Canadian Centre for Policy Alternatives contained very useful data on culture, as did the January 1994 article in *Policy Options*, "Federal Policy and Canadian Magazines," by the Canadian Magazine Publishers Association's Catherine Keachie and policy consultant Kim Pittaway. Again, *Inside U.S. Trade* was a source of up-to-date information. We also quote from *Wired to Win*, the interim report of the Subcommittee on Communications of the Standing Senate Committee on Transport and Communications. We wish also to acknowledge the excellent work of journalists Doug Saunders, Robert Everett-Green, and Laura Eggertson of *The Globe and Mail*, Peter Morton and John Geddes of *The Financial Post*, John Schofield of *Maclean's*, Rosemary Speirs and Shawn McCarthy (then) of *The Toronto Star*, and Giles Gherson and Chris Cobb of the Ottawa *Citizen*.

NOTES

CHAPTER SEVEN: The Eclipse of Political Rights

The framework for this chapter is drawn from David Schneiderman's article in the *University of Toronto Law Journal* (no. 46, 1996), "NAFTA's Takings Rule: American Constitutionalism Comes to Canada." Michael Mandel's analysis of how Canadian corporations are using the Charter of Rights and Freedoms to secure their "rights" as "citizens" is outlined in his chapter on "Rights, Freedoms, and Market Power: Canada's Charter of Rights and the New Era of Global Competition," in *The New Era of Global Competition: State Policy and Market Power* (Montreal and Kingston: McGill-Queen's University Press, 1991), edited by Daniel Drache and Meric S. Gertler. The analysis of the Agreement on Internal Trade is drawn from Maude Barlow's *Straight Through the Heart* (chapter nine) and Tony Clarke's *Silent Coup* (chapter four). These two works also provide the backdrop for the section on "The Big Business Agenda," particularly the role of the BCNI. The sections on "Quebec Sovereignty" and "Provincial Powers" are reflections on the constitutional implications of new investment and trade regimes in the light of the foregoing analysis. The discussion of Ottawa's proposed amendments to the Indian Act and their implications for aboriginal self-government under an MAI regime are drawn from several documents, including *Fiscal Transfers, Programs and Services: The End of the Line?* prepared for the Assembly of First Nations, September 1996; and *Analysis of the Proposed Indian Act Amendments*, prepared by legal analyst Roger Jones, September 1996. The legal and constitutional problems posed by the investor-state mechanism in the MAI were initially spelled out in the report by Robert Stumberg and others to the Western Governors Association in the U.S.

CHAPTER EIGHT: We Can Say No

Trade lawyer Barry Appleton's professional advice on general and country-specific reservations was very helpful for this chapter; we also thank him for pointing out the weakness of including environment and labour standards in the preamble to the MAI. Again we used Barbara Robson's analysis with gratitude.

INDEX

Valenti, Jack, 132
Venezuela, 90

wage disparities, 70–71
Wallach, Lori, 2
Washington Consensus, 14–15, 27, 52, 58; opposition to, 20
water and sewer systems, municipal, 89
Western Governors Association, 161
Westinghouse, 132
White Paper on Employment and Income, 57
Wilson, Michael, 128
Winfield, Mark, 80
Wired to Win: Canada's Competitive Position in Communications, 129–30, 140
women, 74, 105, 116
workfare, 114–15
World Bank, 12, 17, 24

World Investment Report, 19
World Trade Organization (WTO), 2, 25–26, 28; Agreement on the Application of Sanitary and Phytosanitary Measures, 98–99; and broadcasting, 138; and cultural exclusions, 133; and deregulation, 81, 83–84; Financial Services Agreement, 72; and food inspection, 120; and global warming, 90; and MAI, 26, 30–31, 54; and MEAs, 83; ruling on Canadian law protecting magazine industry, 133–34, 137–38; ruling on European ban on North American beef, 97; ruling on U.S. law on gasoline contaminants, 90
World Watch Institute, 76

Zambia, 17